W9-AXP-328

Get Your Sleep On: A no-nonsense guide for busy moms who want to preserve attachment AND sleep through the night.

The Peaceful Sleeper
Christine Lawler, MS, LMFT

Text Copyright © 2021 Christine Lawler

All Rights Reserved

To the tired parents of the world who just want to sleep again without feeling guilty and without screwing up your kids.

And to my beautiful daughters who forced me to read a billion books about sleep training to figure it out. Who now sleep predictably, allowing me to actually write a book.

And to my wonderfully supportive husband, who also happens to be smokin' hot.

And finally, to Otter Pops and Dr. Pepper, because you were there with me every step of the way.

Table of Contents

Introduction

There's nothing in this world like having a baby in your home. It's miraculous. But it's also a ton of work. You're wired and tired. Nobody's getting enough sleep, not even your baby. Maybe you've heard from a friend or you've read on the internet that sleep training can restore the sanity of a full-night's rest to your lives and give you the peace of mind knowing your baby is getting enough sleep as well. But then it turns out there are literally dozens of books and websites that offer contradictory advice on sleep-training a baby, and trying to tackle them all can be an overwhelming task. As a busy mom, you just don't have the time to earn your PhD in sleep training.

Well, I'm here to help you out with all of that. I'm a trained therapist, and I've read the zillions of books, articles, and blog posts on sleep training, so I'm offering you the most concise, informative, "Cliff's Notes" tutorial on sleep training that I can. I've read the big books, so you only need to read this one little book, and you'll be an expert, too.

First, a little about me and why I'm so passionate about all of this:

I'm Christine Lawler. I'm a Licensed Marriage and Family Therapist in Las Vegas. But please call me Chrissy. When I grew up into a "real" professional, I felt like I had

1

to adopt a more formal name, but I've been Chrissy my whole life. When my clients call me "Christine," sometimes I feel like I have to have all my sh*t together. But we're all friends here, so I'll let you in on a little secret: I don't, in fact, always have my sh*t together. Do any of us? So I'm going to kick off my shoes, ease into my yoga pants, grab my Dr. Pepper, and walk through this journey of sleep training (and parenting) with you. This is a no-judgment zone. Get comfortable. I'll be as brief as possible.

I have an amazing husband and four sweet little girls. Like seriously, I hit the jackpot. I've been a therapist for over a decade, and I have an amazing private practice full of clients that I love. I never imagined I'd branch out and write a book like this, but what do you know, here I am.

Why did I do this? I've always been passionate about my own kids sleeping well. It's kind of my "thing." It's made my life better, it's made me a better mom, and it's helped my kids out because they're good sleepers. I kept witnessing wonderful clients and friends around me struggling because of sleep deficits. Eventually I realized, "I have tools to help these people! I know a ton about sleep--I can help moms deal with their anxiety about sleep training." And if sleep is taken care of, all of these other therapeutic issues will improve: Moms will be happier and more well rested. Kids will be calmer, manage emotions better, and have fewer behavioral issues. Marriages will be better because husbands and wives will be able to find some alone time together."

(Sidenote: I can't tell you how many times I've heard people tell me they never have sex anymore because their kids sleep in bed with them. Or they're exhausted and they're never in the mood. Not having sex leads to bigger marital problems. ALWAYS. Marital problems lead to personal problems, etc.)

So for me, writing this book came from a place of passion. I genuinely feel that if people can get sleep managed, almost everything in their lives will run more smoothly. Sleep is an easy and often overlooked solution to a whole host of problems. It doesn't fix everything, but it tones down the magnitude of almost all of life's difficulties.

I want you to see me as your friend. I'm here to take the stress out of sleep training and get everyone in the family a good night's rest. I'm here to help you *enjoy* motherhood--not just endure it. I've helped thousands of parents get great sleep for their little ones. I can help you too! I am so honored to be on this journey with you.

Another side note: there's SO much judgment and mom-shaming out there. Can we please stop that? It's not helpful to anyone. That's my main beef with a lot of the available parenting literature: most parenting books try to establish credibility by essentially saying, "if you don't do it my way, you're wrong, and by the way your kid is going to do drugs and amount to nothing, which will of course be all your fault because you were a crappy parent." Ugh. Let's not.

Read on, friend. I want to help you simplify your life. And even if you don't follow my advice, you're doing fine. We're all doing the best we can for our kids. And guess what? Every parent is different, and every baby is different. I'll give you the basic foundation of universal healthy sleep habits and leave the judgy parts out. Then you can implement sleep training in a way that fits your family. My aim with _The Peaceful Sleeper_ is to help you prioritize sleep and get your little one the rest she needs in a way that fits your family's style. Whether you choose "cry it out" methods or co-sleeping arrangements, I can guide you to better sleep for the whole family. The bottom line is: _sleep is important. How you get there doesn't really matter as long as you do._

Why Sleep Train?

Meeting your baby's sleep needs is one of the most important gifts you can give them. Why? Because sleep promotes physical, emotional, social, and intellectual development.

Let's start off with **WHY** sleep is so important in the first place:

There are somewhere around a bazillion studies out there on the importance of sleep. Other sleep books will spend hundreds of pages distilling all the findings. I'm actually a research nerd, so I find all of this super interesting. But you wouldn't be buying this guide if you wanted to spend hours studying the science. So I'll spare you all the minute details of the research. But I *will* give you the quick-and-dirty "Cliff's Notes" on the major findings:

Think about our very basic needs as human beings: food, sleep, and love are three of our most primal, core needs. We physically cannot survive without them. And we certainly aren't happy when we're deprived of any of them. You don't need me to tell you why food and love are so important. You get that already. And now that you're living with a baby, you probably don't need much convincing that sleep is important too. But just for kicks, I'll give you a few reasons:

Sleep promotes physical, emotional, social, and intellectual development. *Read that one again*. Sleep promotes physical, emotional, social and intellectual development. Isn't that everything you want for your child??

Physical Development
While babies are sleeping, their brains are growing tremendously. Human brains are way more complex than other animals'. Think about horses when they're first born—they can stand up and walk around shortly after birth. Newborn puppies and other mammals crawl to their mothers to nurse. Human babies need much more help and nurturing when they make their entrance. The first three months of a baby's life are often referred to as "the fourth trimester." They sleep most of the time because their brains still have so much growth and development left (Turgeon and Wright 2014, Weissbluth 1999). Our bodies can't physically handle keeping them in the womb any longer, so they have to finish growing in the outside world. My point is, sleep is a time of immense brain development and maturation, which is why babies need tons of it.

Babies' bodies also physically grow and develop during sleep. If you haven't experienced it yet, there will literally be times that you see your baby in the morning and you *know* she's bigger than the day before. You'll also see your baby wake up one morning with a new skill that she didn't have the day before--like smiling or rolling over.

It's pretty cool.

Emotional Development

I don't know about you, but I'm super grumpy when I'm sleep-deprived. But if I'm well-rested--maybe by some miracle I've had the chance to sleep in, I wake up feeling like a million bucks. Likewise, well-rested babies wake up cooing and smiling in the morning, ready to start a glorious and happy day. This is because the brain's emotion centers develop during sleep (Turgeon and Wright 2014). This is even true for children with "spirited" (i.e. "difficult") temperaments (Weissbluth 1999). Sleep helps us regulate our moods and emotions.

Did you know that 80% of individuals with a mental-health diagnosis have a co-occurring sleep problem (Perlis 2016)? 80%! Missing sleep takes a massive toll on emotional regulation that can lead to depression, anxiety, and a whole host of other mental-health issues. The biggest reason I wrote "Get Your Sleep On" was to help families be able to enjoy the precious short time when their child is an infant, free from the stressed-out, brain-fried half-sanity that comes with a lack of sleep.

Social Development

Well-rested kids usually develop faster socially with coos, smiles, laughs and other engaging behaviors (Weissbluth 1999). Again, this in part due to the fact that a full night's rest has given the brain more time to grow and develop. But having their sleep needs met also means babies are happier and more playful. This in turn elicits more social engagement from their caregivers, who aren't as stressed out and overwhelmed, creating an upward cycle of good relationships. It's a lot easier to make friends when you're not always grumpy and sleep-deprived.

Intellectual Development
Well-rested kids are smarter, learn faster, and have lower rates of ADHD and learning difficulties (Sears and Sears 1993). This finding is all over the research. Because babies brains develop when they're sleeping, sleep allows them to make cognitive leaps and bounds. But moms also have more energy to teach kids when everyone is getting a good night's rest. It's easy to let the mind-numbing TV "babysit" kids when you're tired and ragged and just need a nap. Additionally, in our household, we use reading as a main component of our bedtime routine, which is a bonus in fostering intellectual development. I'll get into that more later.

Learning to sleep well is a skill--a VERY important one. It simply isn't as inborn as other milestones our kids achieve effortlessly. We have to work at it. But it's a skill that will benefit your child for literally the rest of his life.

What's keeping you from getting started?

Now we know that sleep is vital. So why all the resistance to sleep training? You've probably heard at least some of the criticism about sleep training. First, let me be clear that sleep training *does not* inherently mean "crying it out." AND "crying it out" doesn't mean ignoring baby at night if he's hungry. I do things differently around here.

Sleep training is about fostering healthy habits and patterns to promote and prioritize sleep with ease. You're training yourself as much as you're training your baby.

Honestly, I think the negative attitudes toward sleep training exist because we spend too much time focusing on why *we*, the adults, want our babies sleep-trained. And then we feel guilty--like we're selfish parents if we aren't sacrificing everything for our kids, including our sanity. And sleep training *feels* selfish because everyone in the home benefits from it, including you. But here's the thing: your baby is the one who actually benefits the most from sleep training. You're doing it for her. You've just read the amazing benefits to her well-being. Plus, when you're well rested, you're a better parent. You take better care of yourself, you're more patient, you're more responsive to her needs, and you have more to give because your tank is full.

If you're married and/or have other kids, the whole family wins when mom's well rested. You may not even notice the fatigue anymore, but it's likely taking a toll. When your hubby starts loving on you at the end of the day, do you mentally throw daggers at him? Do you find yourself being snappy with that toddler of yours who just. won't. obey? No judgment. I've totally been there. When you're well-rested, you're a better version of yourself. Everyone benefits. It's not selfish.

The other common obstacle to sleep training occurs when a baby *protests* sleep. "Protesting" is a therapist's way of saying "baby is pissed because he doesn't think he wants to sleep." As parents, we're conditioned to do anything and everything to keep our kids happy. An unhappy child looks like a big red flag--like mother nature is communicating through his emotions that we're harming him somehow.

But just because your baby doesn't immediately appear to be a willing participant, it doesn't mean he doesn't need sleep. He does. Regardless of what sleep-training option you choose (allowing for crying or not), your baby will protest or resist sleep at some point, in some way. He just wants to stay up and experience all the excitement life has to offer. Kids are notorious for wanting things that aren't good for them. (Aren't we all, to some degree?)

Babies don't know what's best for themselves, which is why, as parents, we have to make the hard calls and enforce rules they don't always like. Have you ever put safety plugs in an electrical socket to keep her from sticking her fingers in it? Or run after your toddler when he's headed for the street, only to have him melt down like you're the meanest person in existence for not letting him do what he wants? What about those excruciating car rides when your baby is pissed that she's in her car seat and cries the whole time? I've had many tear-filled car trips (my baby's tears *and* mine), but it certainly wouldn't be a justification to let her ride unbuckled, would it? No. Did it damage her attachment when you kept her buckled? No. Will she eventually get the hang of it and stop crying when she's in the car? Yes.

Your baby *needs* sleep, and in most cases she's protesting from want, not need. She'll get the hang of it, and she'll eventually enjoy falling asleep. As parents, we don't back down from helping our kids be healthy and safe just because they don't like it. If we know *why* we're doing it, the temporary pain has a purpose.

*Note: If you choose a sleep-training option that allows for some crying, the temporary pain will mostly be yours, as listening to your baby cry and not rushing to comfort her goes against every parental instinct. She may be upset as she protests, but as long as you train her thoughtfully, this will not damage her secure attachment or leave her feeling abandoned or alone. Your baby actually isn't as stressed out as you are. We'll talk more about that in a minute.

If you choose a no-cry option, your emotional pain will be different. You won't be listening to your baby cry, but you will be investing more time in helping him fall asleep when he is resisting. This may be mentally and emotionally taxing and cause you to sacrifice other activities. Many parents choose no-cry sleep solutions initially but later find themselves exasperated as the baby's sleep resistance gets stronger and parental energy diminishes. Please understand that it's okay to switch gears at that point. Figuring out the best sleep solution for your family is a process.

Attachment

Now let's talk about attachment. As I mentioned earlier, when babies vocally protest sleep, many parents get uncomfortable--they worry about their baby's *attachment,* which is the bond that forms between an infant and her caregiver in order for her to feel safe in the world and set the stage for her to form happy and healthy adult relationships. So, let's explore this touchy subject for a minute.

Lots of parents hesitate to let their baby cry it out because they're afraid it will damage their relationship with the baby. These fears are misguided. You don't have to choose a cry-it-out method... but don't avoid it because you're afraid it will harm your baby emotionally.

Attachment is all about being responsive to your baby's needs. Attachment forms when your baby learns she can count on you. When she needs you, you are there. That's how she learns that she is safe and protected in the world. When it comes to sleep, we have to remember that baby's *needs* and her *wants* are different. She does actually *need* to sleep, she just doesn't really want to right now. I can relate to that feeling, can't you? Hello, Saturday-night Netflix binge! You can think of this as the baby version of FOMO (fear of missing out). She's realizing how cool you are and that she'd rather stay up and hang out with you than sleep.

Attachment is a trusting relationship we work on all day (and all night) long. Extreme cry-it-out methods got a bad rap because they ignored other cues about babies' needs and promoted a one-size-fits-all approach that didn't sit well with many loving parents. But that doesn't mean "crying it out" is inherently anti-attachment. Your baby is going to protest sleep training, but your attachment can stay intact. Again, you don't have to let him cry it out. But don't avoid it because you are worried about damaging your child emotionally.

Sleep training really begins the moment babies wake up in the morning. In fact, **effective sleep training has very little to do with how much you let your baby cry when you put her in the crib.** That's why I can confidently say that I help people with any parenting perspective achieve happier, longer sleep.

Effective, long-lasting sleep training is about helping your child learn to self-soothe, prioritizing sleep, fostering family habits conducive to good sleep, and tuning in to your baby to respond to her needs and most of her wants. There is no one-size-fits-all method because all babies and all parents are different. But there are some universal truths we can incorporate. And there actually is no such thing as a "no cry" method--all babies will protest sleep at some point, and all babies cry. My aim is to help you diminish the tears (for baby *and* mom) and get your family sleeping through the night, every night.

14

Attachment-Based Sleep Training

Crying it out sucks. Let's not fool ourselves. But it's also incredibly effective, short-lived and not inherently damaging, even though some would have you believe otherwise.

Preserving a healthy attachment is critical. So is getting good, regular sleep. These two ideas aren't mutually exclusive. Here are five major points to keep in mind to maintain a healthy attachment with your baby as you sleep train:

1. **Understand that crying doesn't always signal an unmet need.** Crying has many purposes. It's basically the only mode of communication an infant has for the first few months. Babies cry when they have needs, when they have wants, when they are protesting, and sometimes they just cry for crying's sake. It's good to be tuned into your baby's cries in order to meet his needs when he has them. Sometimes you can even anticipate his needs. For example, you might recognize that it's been 2.5 hours since he last ate and know he'll probably be hungry soon. As soon as he makes a face or squawks, you know exactly what he wants, and you give it to him before he's upset.

However, we don't need to make it our life's mission or the mark of "good parenting" to shield babies from all crying. Collectively, we have so much parental anxiety about being perfect when our little bundles of joy are so tiny. And that's a good thing. But we go overboard sometimes. When your three-year-old is throwing a fit at the grocery store because she wants candy, you don't feel guilty when you redirect her and move on. You know her want is different than her need. Babies protest too. It's a learning process to decipher needs vs wants when her only mode of communication is crying. So first, learn the difference between needs and wants. Make it your mission to meet her needs as best you can, as often as you can. And remember that one of her greatest needs is sleep! Don't feel guilty about giving your baby predictable sleep times. Really, she craves that kind of structure and consistency. Your baby will gladly go down for naps and go to bed without a fight once she is fully sleep-trained.

2. **Learn to distinguish your own "stuff" from what the baby actually needs.** What's your "stuff"? Oh, you know, the mountain of pressure and expectations you put on yourself to be the most perfect, loving, nurturing, responsive parent ever so that your baby can have a secure attachment and all of the amazing benefits of that.

You want everything good in life for your child. But oftentimes we have to keep our parental guilt in check and discern whether we're actually acting more out of guilt about being perfect or out of a sincere desire to do what's best for our babies. I can't tell you how many times I've heard "I can't let my baby cry at all because it breaks my heart!" Those sentiments, though well-intentioned, are holding your baby back.

3. **Focus on building a secure attachment with your little one *during the day*.** Spend time with him. Put your phone down. Talk to him even if you feel like an idiot because he isn't old enough to talk back yet. Read books to him, take him on walks, and get to *know* him. You'll start to pick up on cues, you'll discern what's going on in his little world, and you'll start to understand his needs and wants. Strive to meet all of his needs and most of his wants. Secure attachment comes from consistently meeting your baby's needs and engaging with him in a loving, responsive way. You'll have times that you totally blow it, when you didn't pick up on a cue, and you will feel awful. But remember that secure attachments are resilient, and they develop just like every relationship--over time and over thousands of encounters. If you are responsive to your baby throughout the day and you meet her need for sleep, letting her cry during sleep training will not damage your attachment with her. She'll already

know that when she's needs you, you're there. And she'll come to realize she doesn't need you to fall asleep. "Crying it out" doesn't usually last more than a couple of days. The more you know and understand her, the more easily you'll be able to know when to make an exception if she's not going to sleep easily. (Yes, of course there are exceptions! We don't just cry it out, no matter what. We will get to the exceptions.)

4. **Establish a predictable routine for naps and bedtime.** Having a consistent and predictable routine signals to baby that sleep is approaching, and she can begin to unwind and prepare for sleep. My bedtime routine includes a bath and lotion, but otherwise it almost exactly mirrors naptime routine. I tell baby it's time to go "night night," then give her a fresh diaper, read stories, then feed, sing a song, and put her in bed. Feeding as the last component before bed contradicts some popular ideologies which counsel parents to let kids eat, then play, then sleep. Many people worry that letting a baby nurse herself to sleep creates a crutch for her. But there is a difference between nursing *before* sleep and nursing *to* sleep. Eating is comforting and relaxing. It can easily be part of your sleep routine without becoming a crutch. Simply feed her and put her in bed. If she falls asleep while nursing, just put her in bed. She'll probably stir when you transfer her. If she's had a full meal,

don't nurse her again to get her to fall back asleep. Just put her down and let her learn to self-soothe. I know, I know--it's easier to nurse again and hope she conks out for good this time. But that's what creates a nursing crutch to sleep, and I promise -the older she gets, the more difficult it will become to nurse her to sleep.

5. **Be consistent.** If you let her cry it out for an hour one night, 10 minutes the next, and 45 minutes the next, she won't understand the rhyme or reason of it, and she'll keep crying to figure it out. This is called variable reinforcement, and it will prolong her protesting. I will explain the different options for crying in a bit so you can figure out what will work best for you and your baby. But whatever option you choose, be consistent about it so your baby can quickly learn what to expect from you.

Sleep Tips by Age

How much sleep does my baby need? Babies need way more sleep than you do, so use these guides as a rough estimate to see how much sleep to expect at various ages

How much sleep does my baby need?
Between four and five months, your baby will need about four naps per day. He should wake up for the day between 6 and 8 am and take his **first nap one to two hours after awakening**. The younger your babe, the shorter the awake time will be. I usually start to notice sleepy cues for 4-month-olds about 75-90 minutes after awakening. This will be the first nap to develop predictably. Naps at this age usually only last an hour, but let baby sleep as long as he wants. No need to wake babies unless naps are going longer than three hours. In general, a good schedule at this young age is one-hour nap, 90 minutes awake and repeat until bedtime. Shoot for bedtime between 6 and 7 pm. **Yes, bedtime should be that early**.

As baby gets closer to 6 months you may start to notice naps and desired awake time start to lengthen. At this point, shoot for awake times closer to 90 to 120 minutes after awakening. Aim for the first nap about 90 min after he wakes for the day. His second nap is usually around noon, and his third nap is typically around 3 pm.

At around nine months, the late afternoon nap disappears, and the midday nap shifts slightly later. If your baby was taking her second nap at noon, shift it to 1:30 or 2:00. Keep the first morning nap about two hours after awakening.

Your baby will hold onto two naps a day until about 16 months, at which point she'll drop the morning nap. You may have to shift naptime again and move the single nap to 12 or 1:00.

Here is a sample schedule for your reference. You may have already noticed that your little one doesn't automatically follow all of the rules in the parenting books. She might meet milestones (roll over, sit up, smile for the first time) earlier or later than what the books dictate. You may be surprised when she doesn't cut her first tooth exactly when she's "supposed" to. Heck, I bet she wasn't even born on her due date. It's no different with this chart. All babies march to the beat of their own drum, so please know that your baby's day may deviate from the exact hours on listed on this chart, and that's fine. If your baby wakes for the day at 6 am instead of 7:30, his first nap will be at 7:30 instead of 9:00 (and it will probably be a long nap). But I want you to have this chart, so you can at least see what her *general* sleep patterns should look like.

Age	0-3 Months	4-9 months	9-16 months	16-24 months	2-3 years	3 years +
Wake up	6-8 am	7:30 am	7:30 am	7:30 am	7:30 am	7 am
1st nap	All naps are totally inconsistent and	9 am	9 am	12:30 pm	12:30 (but may start to drop naps)	
2nd nap	unpredictable	12 pm	2pm			
3rd nap		3pm				
Bedtime	10-11 pm	6:30 pm	6:30 pm	7 pm	8 pm	8pm

Here's another simple reference chart to see averages for babies at different ages. Please note that all babies are different. For example, my babies usually sleep 13-14 hours at night and consequently don't nap for stretches quite as long as those depicted on the chart, but they still meet their optimum sleep average each day.

Age	Number of Naps	Average Hours of DAYTIME Sleep	Average Hours of NIGHTTIME Sleep	Average Hours of TOTAL Sleep
0-2 months	3-5	6-8	9-10*	16-18
2-4 months	3-4	4-5	10-11*	15-16
4-6 months	3	3 ½ - 4 ½	11-12*	14-16
6-9 months	2-3	3-4	11-12	14-15
9-12 months	2	2 ½ - 3 ½	11-12	14-15
12-18 months	1-2	2-3	11-12	13-14
18-24 months	1	1 ½ - 2 ½	11-12	13-14
2-3 years	1	1-2	11-12	12-13
3-5 years	0-1	0-1	10-11	10-11

*Interrupted for nighttime feedings

If your little one's averages are way different than what you see here, contact me for a consultation and we'll determine how to make tweaks.

Preventing Overtiredness

Before we get into different sleep-training approaches, we *must* talk about the absolute biggest factor in sleep training: preventing overtiredness. Remember how I said earlier that sleep training really isn't about whether or not you let the baby cry after you put him in bed? Well, are you ready for this? **Sleep training *is* about preventing overtiredness.** This is the biggest secret, divulged. This is the cornerstone of happy, blissful sleep.

It may seem counterintuitive, but the more your baby sleeps, the more she will sleep. Sleep begets sleep. The biggest mistake parents make when it comes to sleep for their babies is underestimating how much they actually need and when they need it.

Overstimulation: their Achilles heel

Babies easily can get overstimulated. Remember how undeveloped their cute little brains are? When there's too much going on, they don't know how to handle it, and they freak out. Instead of shutting down and sleeping like they should, they get wired and they *can't* sleep.

We've probably all made those classic mistakes with newborns where we had a big day and our sleepy little babe was wide awake for, let's say, five hours. We thought it was so much fun, and they were so happy!

And then…. then later they absolutely lose their sh*t. You're so confused because you can't get them to calm down, they're not falling asleep, and they're SCREAMING. That's overstimulation. A newborn shouldn't have any stretches of awake time that long.

I have this horrible memory of taking my oldest to a Rangers game when she was two months old. She slept easily on the go, my husband loves baseball, and I hate to miss a party, so I took my baby wrap and confidently strutted into the stadium. I assumed she'd fall asleep wrapped to me, and I could hang out and watch the game with friends. Baseball is a pretty quiet sport, after all.

Facepalm.

It was horrendous. Baseball in a stadium?! Not quiet at all. What my adult brain could tune out (all the music, the loud announcer, the bright lights), my little baby could not. She didn't sleep a wink. At first, she LOVED it! She was happy and having fun, and my husband beamed that he'd have a little baseball sidekick when she got bigger. Oh, but then… No. She was not having fun. That easy-tempered baby screamed and hollered like I'd never heard before. And I spent the next few innings walking around outside the stadium bouncing and "shhh"-ing and nursing and trying every trick I had to get her to calm down. Then I called it quits on the game, picked a fight over nothing with my husband on the car ride home because I was so agitated and stressed out, and I cried too. All while she was still screaming in the back seat.

Never again.

That was my lesson about overstimulation. Well, one of them. It's surprising what can be overstimulating at unexpected times. Activities like going shopping, taking a walk, or interactions with toddlers and older kids might normally be fine, but sometimes they might overstimulate babies. Essentially anything that gets a baby brain to choose to stay awake instead of choose to go to sleep is overstimulating. Newborns have a strong sleep drive that usually overpowers the urge to experience the excitement. Usually. This is why it's important to be mindful of sleep times/patterns. If your baby isn't falling asleep amidst the excitement when she usually would, you know to intervene and get her somewhere dark and quiet.

Around three to four months of age, that strong newborn sleep drive wears off, and your baby will be able to stay awake more. That's when it becomes your job, Mama, to take him away from the excitement and provide an environment conducive to sleep. It takes some trial and error and getting to know your baby as he's navigating all of this. That's why four to five months is the prime time for sleep training. You can figure out his patterns and give him a predictable schedule right when his sleep drive is still pretty strong and he's acquired some self-soothing skills.

By four to five months, she's not as susceptible to overstimulation anymore because her brain is more developed, but she can get *overtired*, which is closely related.

Prevent overtiredness by giving adequate sleep throughout the day:

Starting the day off right is your biggest asset, beginning with the first nap. **Between four and 16 months of age, your baby needs her first nap within one to two hours of waking up.** Yes, you read that right. Even if baby just woke up from 12 solid hours of night sleep, she needs to go back down about 90 minutes after she wakes up. Babies younger than 9 months usually need 90 minutes of awake time or less first thing in the morning. Babies closer to 16 months can probably handle 2-2.5 hours. But keep a close eye on your babe to see what *his* ideal awake time is.

The optimal time to put your baby to sleep is *before* she starts acting tired. We often think that rubbing eyes and fussing signal tiredness, but those are actually signs of being overtired. You want to look for more subtle cues, e.g. when your baby starts to become quiet and movement slows. Eyes may drift, she's less engaged, she yawns, and her activity level has decreased. My youngest will start to get a pink hue on her eyelids when she's sleepy and she might utter one little fuss here and there.

If you can get your baby to bed when this starts

happening, she'll drift off really easily. Babies struggle more when they're overtired. Their brains get wired, and it's harder for them to calm down and soothe to sleep. (This happens to big kids and adults too. We call it a second wind.)

Side note: babies often have a dawn awakening, which trips lots of parents up. This is a super-early-morning awakening between 4:30 and 6:00 am. **This is NOT your baby's time to wake up for the day.** It's very normal for your baby to have a wakeful period then, but just feed her and put her back to bed (or if she's just playing, leave her be). Your baby should arise for the day between 6 and 8 am. If you let her get up and stay up in the wee hours of the morning, 5 am will become her permanent start to the day. No, no, no. We don't want that. You both will be worn out by the end of the day. If you consistently put her back to bed at that point (even if she seems cheerful and ready to party for the day), she'll learn to fall back asleep and to sleep in later.

My first two kids went to bed at 6 pm every night after they were sleep-trained at five months. So when they woke up at 5 am to eat, I figured they were legitimately hungry after 11 hours of fasting. But they held onto that early morning feeding until I weaned them from it at 12 months. Physically, after about nine months, they didn't need to eat--it was just a habit. And at 5 am it was easier to feed them and go back to bed than it was to worry about weaning them from that feeding.

When I had my third and fourth babies, I was well into

my work as a sleep consultant, and I'd already written the first version of this book. So, they are the best (and most recent) examples of me implementing my principles with purpose and not just "winging it" like I had with the first two.

I sleep trained my third baby right at 4 months and she was definitely the easiest! She usually goes to bed between 6-6:30 and wakes up at 7am. At 7 months, she dropped the dawn feeding all by herself. My fourth baby just turned 6 months. We sleep trained her at 4 months as well, and she hasn't dropped the night feeding yet but she does occasionally. I know she's close. She typically sleeps from 7pm-8am with one feed.

One thing you might try to eliminate that dawn feeding is a tactic called a "dream feed". This means feeding your baby three hours after he's fallen asleep at night. He'll still be so drowsy that he'll drift right back to sleep afterward (or may not even fully awaken while eating). If you're using formula, give your baby the same amount as usual. If you're nursing, try pumping since baby will likely drink more from a bottle when drowsy. Or you can choose to supplement with formula here to ensure a good, full meal. Supplementing for one feeding won't impact your supply, and oftentimes you aren't producing much breast milk late at night anyway. If the dream feed isn't offsetting any other awakenings after trying it for a few days, drop it because it's not helping.

*Full disclosure: I could never get a dream feed to work.

It felt like I was disturbing her sleep more by waking her up to feed her. It definitely didn't help anything, but frankly, it seemed to make things worse. Some mamas rave about it, so I still want to mention it in case it's good for you.

Naps should last one to two hours. As a general rule, a nap that lasts less than 45 minutes isn't enough--unless it's the third nap of the day. Sometimes babies stir and fall back asleep at the halfway point of their nap. I call that a nap-intruder, and your best bet is to allow 30 minutes for baby to fall back to sleep. He'll learn put himself back to sleep and eventually stop waking up at that 45-minute mark. If he wakes up crying, that's generally a sign that his frontal lobe is still shut down, and he's not done sleeping. He should wake up in a good mood, cooing and playing happily in his crib.

If naps are consistently short or it's taking forever to fall asleep, try adjusting the amount of time baby is awake between naps. Start first with shortening the awake window and if that doesn't work, then lengthen it. It sounds counterintuitive to put your baby to sleep *earlier* when she's already struggling to fall asleep, but this really works--babies fight sleep when they're overtired, not undertired.

Try your best not to mess with sleep times, especially in the first few months. Don't keep your baby up past his nap- or bedtimes, and don't rely on letting him nap in the car. Even if your child seems to be a great car sleeper, the quality of his sleep is poor in the car. Don't count on him being flexible with naps until about 12 months. At that time, when his sleep has become predictable, he can occasionally handle going down an hour later. But in those early months, if your baby usually naps from 8:30-10 and you don't get him down until 9:30, he might only sleep for 30 minutes. Or worse, he may just cry for 30 minutes and refuse to nap. If you mess with his sleep window, sometimes you miss it. And he probably won't ever make up for all of the missed sleep. Even if by some miracle he gets the full-length nap, the subsequent naps and bedtime get thrown off. It's just not worth it.

In the first year, bedtime should be early. Shoot for 6-7 pm. My girls had a 6:00 bedtime until they were 9-12 months old. I know, it sounds so early. But then you have an entire evening to spend with your spouse to keep your relationship alive. You can also relax, do some self-care, and get caught up on other chores. It's hard if you work and your baby has to go to bed as soon as you get home. But she needs her sleep. (I know--she needs her mama too. See if you can arrange an earlier work schedule with your boss. Maybe you can go in at 7 or 8 am and come home earlier.)

Why so early? They just sleep better when they go down earlier. There's way less protesting and over-tiredness. Babies get their best sleep before midnight, so I like to maximize those hours. Also, as they grow they usually stay up later but wake up at the same time. If you start off with a later schedule, you run the risk of having bedtime battles AND morning battles with your toddler as you try scooting her schedule up.

Some parents really want to make a later bedtime work. By all means, try it. If you really want a 9pm-9am schedule you can try to have your schedule shifted. But please tune in and be responsive to baby's needs. Some babies are flexible sleepers and can have a schedule like that. Many just can't. If your baby isn't doing well with an adjusted schedule, move it earlier.

The other wrench that gets thrown in here is the weekend and your social life. 6 pm is awfully early to turn in on a Saturday night. Stay tuned later for tips on preserving sleep *and* having a social life.

How to Sleep Train

Alright, let's do this! I've inspired you (hopefully) to know that sleep training holds the promise of health and happiness, and now you want to jump in.

First of all, you've got to choose a methodology for the right reasons--because your baby needs her sleep. Go re-read the chapter titled "Why Sleep Train?" if you need to. This will motivate you to stick with your program and do it right. Crying it Out (CIO) got a bad reputation is because some people misunderstood how to do it (the baby was overtired, there was no bedtime routine, and they let her cry no matter what). Decide on a method, and learn how to implement it best. Each option has its pros and cons. And remember, letting your baby cry doesn't make you a bad parent. If implemented properly, you are actually letting your child learn invaluable self-soothing tools and reducing lots of tears in the long run.

You've also got to be prepared for the barriers to sleep training so you can push through them. Each method will take a while to produce obvious benefits. It's normal to feel exasperated and want to give up. Don't. When it's 1 am and the baby is crying, it's a helluva lot easier to just bring him into your bed so everyone can go right back to sleep. I've been there. I get it. The thing is, what's easier when you're dead-tired at zero-dark-early is SO much more work (and so much less sleep) in the long run.

Once you've got your reasons, your method, and your plan, then your job is to be consistent in following through. I recommend implementing your plan perfectly for two full weeks before you conclude it isn't working and try something different. Having a detailed sleep log is crucial. Our ability to keep the facts straight and our analysis objective is radically diminished when we're under stress. Plus, it's reassuring to remind yourself there actually has been measurable progress.

I was the sleep training ringleader in our house, and with my first two kids, my husband turned to me, exasperated, around day 10 and said, "Babe, this isn't working. What should we do?" to which I replied, "Yes, it is! Go look at the chart." Sure enough, I was right (obviously), and by day 14 we really had established a predictable rhythm. Our baby was going to sleep without protesting and waking up happy and rested. So was I. Glory, glory.

After you've got a schedule figured out, stick to it. Sleep is your number-one priority with regard to your baby's development. And preventing overtiredness is your secret weapon. You will make sacrifices to preserve sleep. But remember, you're doing this for your baby, and the long-term payoffs are gigantic.

Let's get to your three main options:

Sleep-Training Options

There are three main approaches to sleep training: Extinction or "Cry It Out" (CIO), Ferber Method or "Modified Crying it Out", and "No-Cry." What you choose basically depends on your level of tolerance for crying, your consistency, your parenting style, and your baby.

I chose "Cry it Out" for my first two babies and "Modified Crying it Out" for my third and fourth. Each time it was quick, easy, and relatively painless. They've been fantastic sleepers ever since, and I know without a doubt that allowing for crying was the right option for us. But I'm not here to pressure anyone or make you feel like that's the only style for you. If you don't choose CIO, that's totally fine. But I do want to set the record straight about CIO when I say it's not anti-attachment. You're not going to damage your baby or your relationship if you cry it out.

The *Cliff's Notes* on each option:

Cry it Out: When your baby is clean, fed, isn't overtired, and you've had a warm and nurturing naptime/bedtime routine, you put him in the crib and lovingly and calmly walk out of the room, even if he protests. You can reassure him as you go, but you leave. Set your timer for one hour. If your baby still isn't asleep by the end of that hour, I recommend rocking to sleep. For older babies who are more resilient protestors some parents will choose to cry it out for longer than an hour. But I find that even if you have to rock to sleep after an hour of fussing you can still get results within a few days. I think one of the reasons "sleep training" gets a bad rap is because we hear some parents say "my baby screamed for 3 hours the first night but then the second night only screamed for 2 hours and it got less and less. Sleep training is awesome!" While some parents have success that way, it really doesn't have to be that intense. Usually the babies that protest so much are those that are overtired.

For naps we also want to give them an hour to fuss and then rock to sleep if they haven't fallen asleep on their own. When they're young we usually want to save the nap so they're not just stacking overtiredness on overtiredness.

- Put your baby down for her regular three to four naps during the day
- Interact with your baby and meet her needs throughout the day
- Establish a consistent bedtime routine
- Put her down at a regular time (6-7 pm) each night, verbally reassure her with familiar language ("Night-night! It's time to sleep!"), and walk out of the room for 60 minutes
- If, after that hour baby hasn't fallen asleep, rock to sleep

Modified Crying (also called "Check and Console" or "the Ferber Method"): Instead of letting her cry until she calms herself, you set a timer and go in to help soothe after set intervals. With this method, you do 10-15-20-20-20-minute intervals. In my experience sleep training thousands of babies, I find that most babies with a solid sleep foundation set as newborns fall asleep in that first or second twenty-minute timer.

Many parents choose this option because they want to console their baby and offer comfort along the way. I used to prefer strict Cry It Out. Now I prefer Modified Cry it Out with a few tweaks I added along the way.

Traditional "Ferber Method" says to just offer verbal reassurance when you do your checks and maybe pat baby's bum or stroke her cheek in the crib but don't pick her up. This totally backfired for my children and made them more upset. This is why I chose strict Cry It Out with my first two kids.

Instead, I say after your timers go in and help baby get calm in whatever way works. (But I would refrain from offering a breast to calm since baby has just eaten prior to going down). Pick him up, rock, shush, offer the pacifier, whisper verbal reassurances, do a cheek or eyebrow stroke, etc. When your baby is calm, set him back in the crib and start your next timer when he starts crying.

If, by the end of that third 20-minute timer, he still

hasn't fallen asleep yet then just rock him to sleep.

The most important thing to note when you are doing any version of Cry It Out is the variability in the level of crying. This can teach you a lot about your baby and help you track their soothing progress. I like to use a scale from 0-10 to rate crying where zero is totally calm and quiet and 10 is absolutely losing his mind. Any time baby de-escalates on his own, he's putting a piece of the "self-soothing puzzle" into place. Even if he goes from a level 7 crying to a 4 to a 6 to a 3, those are steps in the right direction. If he cries at a level 8 and then drops down to a level 3, even if it's just for 10 seconds, that's a small win.

Modified Cry it Out in a nutshell:

- Essentially the same as CIO
- The only difference is that when he cries, you set timers and come back to offer reassurance and calming at specified intervals
- Ten minutes for the first stretch, 15 minutes the second, and then three 20-minute intervals
- Some babies end up protesting more with this approach, but I find it works best for the majority of babies and caregivers.

*Remember, we are helping babies learn self-soothing in this process. Self-soothing is a critical skill we want our children to have for life. This is not cruel abandonment and teaching our babies that we are unresponsive.

Some who oppose cry it out argue that we are allowing their system to get overrun by the stress hormone, cortisol. While it is true that cortisol is produced when crying, there are about a million things our babies and children will endure that will cause crying and cortisol production. I.e., getting baby dressed, wiping boogers, buckling in a car seat, tummy time, vaccinations, bonks and faceplants when learning to walk and crawl, etc. The most important part of what we're doing is helping our babies learn to de-escalate and *regulate* their cortisol.

Many parents report that after sleep training they have a "totally different baby." "He's so happy now. He's all smiles and we have a completely different relationship!"

No-Cry: In theory this sounds like the option everyone would want. But basically "no cry" means you soothe your baby as much as he wants until he falls asleep. Once you have a good foundation of long naps and easy sleep initiation, you can scale back the level of intervention required to get baby to sleep so he's doing the sleep initiation more independently over time. So the "sleep training" part of it focuses on scheduling, establishing a good sleep environment, and getting into good sleep patterns. Mom's involvement helping her baby getting to sleep is very high and stays that way longer-term. It's a lot of work for mom, but many moms don't mind that. This is a popular option for first-time moms who don't have other kids or demands on their time and can afford to spend that extra time with their baby.

- Establish the same routines for nap- and bedtimes and meeting needs throughout the day as you would with the other two options
- With this method, you will be present with your baby as she falls asleep--you will help soothe her to sleep (through nursing, cuddling, etc.) as she awakens throughout the night
- No-cry method requires quite a bit more effort from caregivers to implement, it often involves co-sleeping, and it may take months or even years before your baby is fully sleeping through the night
- Please be aware of safety and relational hazards that come with co-sleeping, and make plans to circumvent them before choosing this option

Now, I'll give you a little more detail about all three options, so you can choose what will work best for your family:

For all sleep training options, you'll want to make sure your baby is clean, fed, and isn't overtired. Again, optimal bedtime for babies four to 12 months old is between 6 and 7 pm.

Good sleep actually starts when a baby first wakes up in the morning. Remember that it's important to put your baby down for her first nap within one to two hours of wakefulness. I promise that preventing overtiredness is the key to smooth sleep training, so I'm saying it again. And again.

Extinction or Crying it Out (baby must be older than four months)

Classic CIO means first making sure that all of a baby's needs are met, and then leaving her alone in her crib to learn how to self-soothe. The first nights/naps are hardest, but in most cases she will get the hang of it in just a few days. Here's what it looks like:

We want to set the stage during the day for optimal sleep training conditions that night. So our top priority is getting baby to nap well on day 1. If you're putting your baby down during that optimal window, within one to two hours of waking for the day and he's not overtired, he'll likely doze in your arms during that last feeding before his nap. Hence, there won't be much crying. If he does cry, **on day one just do whatever you need to do to get baby to nap well, like nursing or rocking him to sleep.** The meat of sleep training happens that night, but you'll set the stage for night one if he is already well-rested.

Subsequent naps on day one will be the same. If he's not overtired, hopefully napping will be smooth, but if he protests, then again do whatever you need to do to give him a good nap. This means on the first day you can hold for all naps if you need to.

After dinner give your baby a nice, warm bubble bath. Play with her, and give her lots of love and attention. Afterwards, massage her with lotion. Use this time to make good eye contact, give lots of smiles and kisses, and play. Put her jammies on, brush her teeth (if she has them), then read her a few stories. Even when she's little, it's so, so beneficial to read to her. I read three to five stories before bed each night. Then turn out the lights, and give her the last feeding. After she's done eating, put her directly in bed. She may fall right to sleep because she's been so relaxed by the last feeding. Or she may jolt to attention at the injustice of being put in her crib. If she starts to protest right away, reassure her verbally as you continue to walk out the door. I always say "I love you so much, sweetie. I love you! It's time to go night-night. Time to go night-night."

Now this is the hard part: you just let her cry, and eventually she'll fall asleep. Most babies will cry for about 30 minutes to an hour that first night. Some resilient protestors will cry hard for more than an hour, and I've even heard of some babies who will protest for as long as two to four hours. But I firmly believe that only happens with babies who are already severely over-tired. As I mentioned before, I like to cap the crying at 60 minutes and then rock to sleep. There's no need to be too intense in this process. Length of protesting depends on how overtired the baby is by bedtime and how long she has had bad habits. If you're doing Cry-it-Out with an 18-month-old, the protesting will be longer than if she were 4 months.

If, after an hour, baby is crying and doesn't seem to be making progress I recommend you go back in and soothe. Feel free to rock to sleep if need be. We'll keep practicing tomorrow. Some worry that going back in after an hour will just teach baby to persist and cry for an hour every night, but I would be surprised if that were actually the case.

You should notice some variability in baby's cries. She may fluctuate between escalated crying, whimpers and some quiet moments. This is a great sign! Every time she de-escalates her crying she is using her new self-soothing skills. She will continue to get better at it!

However long she cries, the next night will generally be shorter. Each night thereafter the protesting will get shorter and shorter. Most babies wake up happy and full of smiles the next day, not batting an eye after the previous night. Some, if they protested for a long time, will be sleep-deprived and emotionally fragile. As with anything, make sure you give her lots of love and attention during the day to keep building a strong attachment.

After that first day, you do the same thing for naps (minus the bath and lotion) and leave your baby for a full hour. If he doesn't fall asleep, either rock him to sleep at that point or get him out and try again at the next naptime. The first three to four days will be hardest, but after that you'll start to see plenty of improvement. Within just a few days, instead of crying at naptime, he'll usually roll around and play and then fall asleep more quickly.

Obstacles (I know, sometimes it's not THAT easy):
- **Limbs caught in crib slats, baby tangled in clothes/blanket/etc:** What if something really is wrong and I make her cry through it (says every parent's guilt when they're starting CIO)?? This is where a <u>video monitor</u> comes in handy. It'll make you feel better if you can know she doesn't have her legs stuck in the bars, isn't tangled up in her clothes, etc.
- **Pooping:** My oldest would poop in protest, and not knowing whether or not she'd soiled herself complicated CIO. If she cried longer than usual (after she was sleep-trained I knew that anything more than five minutes of straight crying or 15 minutes of off-and-on crying was unusual), I'd go in, check her diaper, change it if needed, and put her right back in bed. Eventually she stopped doing it because it didn't really win her any more time out of bed.
- **Puking:** If your baby is the cry-so-hard-they-puke type, you'll have to go in, clean her up, give a quick snuggle, verbal reassurance, and put her right back in bed. She'll stop that behavior if she learns it doesn't give her an advantage, and this is definitely something you want baby to unlearn. For some babies that throw up, strict cry it out

just isn't a great option. Consider doing modified cry it out with shorter intervals.

- **Passing out:** A friend of mine has a little girl who passes out if she starts crying hard. So crying it out wasn't a good option for her, and they all adapted. Note: crying it out might not be for everyone, and that's okay!

- **Waking up to eat**: What about waking up to eat? Depending on his age, your little one may still need to eat in the middle of the night. Between four and six months, he will probably still need one or two feedings a night. If he wakes up to eat, wait 5-10 minutes to let him wake up fully and even get a little worked up. This serves two purposes: 1) if he doesn't need to eat and is just momentarily aroused (we all stir in the middle of the night), just talking and rolling around, you give him the opportunity to fall back asleep on his own if he doesn't need to eat. 2) If he does need to eat, this ensures that he's awake enough to get a full feeding. Put him back in his crib after his feeding and let him fall asleep on his own. (Usually there is no protesting in the middle of the night. If there is in the beginning, it'll end real soon.) Once he is sleep-trained, his night wakings will radically diminish because he knows how to put himself back to sleep, so he'll only wake up when he actually needs to eat.

Check and Console/Modified Crying it Out

For this method, you'll want to have the same structured bedtime routine every night, as discussed above. Again, preventing overtiredness is key. Then, instead of leaving her until morning (or until a midnight feeding) you leave her for ten minutes, then check on her and comfort her. Feel free to pick her up and snuggle her until she is calm. Then, place her back in the crib and set your next timer for 15 minutes. Some babies will calm down while still in the crib if you just gently touch her belly or pat her bum. Don't pick her up unless you need to. Once she is calm, put her right back down and start your next timer when baby starts crying. After 15 minutes, go console baby and set your next timer for 20. Repeat the 20-minute timer 2-3 more times if need be, and then just rock baby to sleep if she hasn't fallen asleep on her own by that point. Each time, tell baby you love her, give reassurances and tell her it's time to go to sleep.

I actually initially chose modified CIO for my firstborn, but I quickly learned that this method wouldn't work for us. I wanted to respond to my baby and be there for her when she needed me, and I thought I'd feel guilty if I let her cry it out. But I underestimated how intense modified CIO would be for us. I'd read that I shouldn't pick her up and should just be there next to the crib telling her I love her. There was *so* much interaction with my agitated baby, and every single minute passed by painfully. She didn't calm when I was in there "soothing" and every time I left, she protested harder. Setting timers and re-subjecting both of us to the heartache of leaving felt unnecessary. After one night, I gave up. Then I read a lot more, armed myself with a plan, and opted to try full Cry it Out the following week.

I don't honestly know how things would have gone if I had tried a more hands on approach to modified cry it out. I do know that consoling her without touching her and picking her up just made us both more upset. She did great with full cry it out and so do many babies.

Sometimes check-and-console methods can take longer for a baby to really get the hang of. At the time I figured I'd rather have two to three really hard nights than one to two still-pretty-hard weeks. And it worked! Instead of the hours I'd spent checking and consoling, she cried for 30 minutes and went right to sleep. I did the same full cry it out method with my second and it worked great.

With my third and fourth babies, "Modified Crying it Out" worked like a charm. I was amazed! She calmed down immediately when I went to console her, often without even picking her up, and she didn't start crying right away when I left. It was a totally different experience.

Every parent and every baby are different, so the "Check and Console" method might fit your style or might work for your baby better! If it works, most parents prefer to start with this option. Mamas can benefit by having structured, set times to go in and help your baby calm down, offer reassurance, and show love.

No-Cry Method

You've probably heard me say before that there's no such thing as a "no cry" method. Babies cry and they protest sleep. It's not our parental mission to avoid all tears. The closest it gets to "no cry" involves a lot of diligence on your part to soothe him to sleep whenever it's naptime/bedtime. Many who choose this option also choose to co-sleep and nurse all night. Keep in mind, with co-sleeping it's tempting to put your baby on a similar schedule to yours and go to bed for the night together. But your baby needs way more sleep than you do. Even if you're co-sleeping, her bedtime should still be 6-7 pm. This method requires more effort than the other options and can take months/years for baby to really get the hang of.

Once you have a solid foundation in place rocking baby to sleep, the aim (for some) is to slowly scale back the level of intervention needed to fall asleep so that baby can eventually do it on his own. Some moms are fine with rocking to sleep and holding for naps long term.

Just like with the other two methods, with "no cry," scheduling and preventing over-tiredness are key. Naptimes should still occur at regular times with a consistent naptime routine. You'll also need to learn to soothe your baby to sleep without always nursing her. This one can get tricky because she may just fall asleep at the breast. If that happens, that's fine. But don't offer her the breast again if she's already full, just to get her to keep sucking. Try offering a pacifier, or just hold her hand or lie next to her as she dozes off. It will be tempting to nurse her to sleep, but eventually you'll stop nursing or be unavailable to nurse to sleep on occasion. Older babies are also way more distractible so relying on nursing to sleep can become frustrating later on. Babies need to learn how to fall asleep another way.

You'll want to determine what you plan to do while your baby is sleeping. Do you plan to lie next to her throughout the entire nap and early bedtime? Or do you plan to stay in the room until she's asleep and then sneak out? If you want to have the freedom to get other things done while she's sleeping, you'll want to make sure you create a little more distance between you two while she's falling asleep. Initially, you may be rocking/holding her while she's sleeping, but this will become more challenging as she gets bigger and heavier. I recommend still putting her to sleep in a crib or in bed and lying down next to her or holding her hand. This resolves your desire to be close, but she doesn't need to be ON you to sleep.

I often compare sleep training to teaching our kids how to go down the slide. In the beginning when they're young, we put them on the top of the slide and hold them all the way down saying "weeee!" As they get older and stronger we slowly scale back the level of intervention: sliding down with them, holding their core as they slide down, holding their hand, giving them a boost and waiting close by, waiting at the bottom of the slide, helping them up the ladder, etc., and then eventually we can hang out over on the bench while they do the slide all by themselves.

"No Cry" sleep training should look like this. As newborns we're helping all babies lay a good foundation and teaching them how to sleep well, with lots of assistance. Then we scale back in phases based on their readiness.

Phase 1: getting on a more predictable schedule, 90 min awake time, 60 min napping. Rock to sleep and hold for naps

Phase 2: rock to sleep, put down, jostle back to sleep if she wakes in the transition.

Phase 3: rock to mostly drowsy, put down, jostle to sleep

Phase 4: rock, put down, hand on chest until she falls asleep

Phase 5: rock to drowsy, put down.... Slowly scale back the level of intervention over time:

Here are some ideas of interventions to try. Get creative!

- Cheek stroke
- Leaning over crib singing songs
- Shushing
- Sitting next to bed
- Sitting in a chair in the room
- Holding paci in place
- Holding finger
- Eyebrow/face stroke
- Lean into the crib and rest cheek to cheek
- Palm on cheek
- Lay on the floor and hold hands through the crib bars
- Lay on the floor quietly or singing songs without touching
- Allowing little bits of fussing

Remember that all babies cry and protest. So the objective of this method isn't to have zero fussing at all, it's that you are THERE with your baby as she is learning and working it out. You are soothing along the way.

Many moms who choose this approach will have moments along the way where they are present with their baby, she's fussing or protesting and they know in their gut that she is fine. She's just working things out and mama's presence isn't adding any additional value. So they choose to step away for small increments of time to see if baby may settle better without distraction. The goal of this sleep training method is to be RESPONSIVE to all of baby's NEEDS. If you determine that you can step away for a moment while still doing that, that's totally fine. You're not going to ruin things by being inconsistent if you give a little more independence at times when you know she can handle it.

Three key practices to keep in mind for successful "no cry" sleep training:

- **Prepare yourself to be patient and flexible:** You cannot always predict how long it will take your little one to fall asleep. Sometimes he'll conk out after five minutes, and sometimes he'll want to roll around and play for 30 minutes. This doesn't mean he wasn't ready for sleep yet, it just means he's got something on his mind and he's learning to relax. If you get frustrated that you don't have control over how long it takes your little one to unwind, the sweet, peaceful moments of watching him drift off to sleep are replaced by overwhelm and frustration.

- **Prepare your mind for the downtime and stillness:** Be intentional about the opportunity to have this sweet time with your baby. With endless to-do lists waiting, some mamas go crazy "doing nothing" while they wait for their baby to fall asleep. Use this time to meditate, daydream, pray, or listen to an audiobook or podcast. If you have things you're looking forward to doing during the stillness, you won't feel stuck there. Sidenote: Beware of consistently napping while the baby naps. I know, "sleep when your baby sleeps" is advice you hear all the time. That is true for the newborn stage, when your sleep is going to be fragmented anyway and you are recovering from pregnancy and childbirth. But you don't need as much sleep as your baby, so if you're napping whenever he is, you'll steal from your ability to sleep well at night, which can lead to chronic insomnia. (If insomnia is already an issue, contact me, because I can fix that too.)

- **Most importantly, don't be fooled by short naps:** A nap that lasts 45 minutes or less does not count. Ideally, naps should be about 60-90 minutes in duration. Sometimes babies wake up briefly mid-nap but aren't done sleeping. If you are resting next to your sleeping babe, you'll be more aware of his stirring and short wakeful periods than if you just had a monitor nearby. Similarly, if your baby is used to falling asleep next to you and then notices you're not there anymore, he may wake up and fuss more often. If he wakes up before he's napped long enough, see if you can get him to fall back to sleep and finish the nap.

There are some great books and resources on "no cry" sleep training, so if this seems like what you are looking for and want additional reading, William Sears, Elizabeth Pantley, James McKenna, and Tracy Hogg are the experts for you (relevant titles are listed in the "Resources" section). Although I fully support you choosing the parenting method that works for you and your baby, I do want to alert you to some downsides to co-sleeping that are worth considering.

Downsides to co-sleeping:

- **Poorer sleep quality for mom and baby.** He may be super cute, snuggly, and peaceful now, but the bigger he gets, the squirmier he'll be. Even if you get used to the wiggling and kicking, your sleep quality is massively impacted. In adult sleep studies, they measure "periodic leg movements," which are basically slight leg or toe twitches that are completely unnoticeable to the sleeper, but bring them out of restorative sleep. If you have a baby bumping into you all night or nursing on demand, it has the same effect as those periodic leg movements (meaning you're not getting the restorative sleep you need). When you're sleep-deprived it can have an effect on your mental/emotional well-being and responsiveness to your baby during the day. To me, the tradeoff isn't worth it.
  - It's also important to take precautions to reduce the risk of SIDS, like making sure your baby sleeps on his back, ensuring there are no cracks or crevices in between the bed and headboard where your baby could get stuck, and safeguarding that you won't accidentally roll over on him in the middle of the night. Those fears alone

made my sleep shallow whenever one of my babies was in bed with me.

- **Reduced intimacy and closeness with partner**. There are *so, so* many ways that a new baby already changes the dynamic of your marriage and shifts your priorities regarding your partner. I don't think it's healthy for your baby to physically come between you every night. Activities like intimacy, cuddles before bed, pillow talk, and middle-of-the-night touching strengthen your marriage in immeasurable ways. It's important to keep the family hierarchy intact, meaning that husband and wife are the central unit and children come second. That may sound harsh, but it's easy to fall out of love if you're not prioritizing each other. Having a strong, connected marriage benefits your baby in thousands of ways. If you do choose to co-sleep, be diligent about preserving closeness and intimacy with your partner.

- **Overdependence on parents**. It's good for your baby to learn independence and self-reliance. As much as you want to, you can't be there for her every second of the day, every day of her life. She needs to learn how to be away from you, how to calm herself down, and how to self-regulate. In my experience, moms who co-sleep have a much harder time leaving their babies with a sitter to go on a date or do something for themselves. Self-care isn't selfish. And your partner needs you too.

Going on dates and mini-vacations without your baby can be a huge boost to your relationship. Going grocery shopping alone or getting a pedicure on occasion can be good for you, too. If your baby can't deal without you, you're not likely to engage in these marriage- and sanity-boosting activities.

All of that being said, I've been doing this long enough to know many families who happily co-sleep and parents who report good sleep quality, great relationship quality and kids who have independence in other aspects of childhood.

Creating a Sleep Log

Whichever method you choose for sleep training, it's helpful to keep a detailed log rather than relying on your own subjective experiences. Facts are helpful to track progress, see improvements, and maintain your sanity.

What is a Sleep Log?

A sleep log is basically a fancy chart. On the x-axis (horizontal) mark a spot for each individual day for 14 days. On the y-axis (vertical) mark each hour of the day.

Then grab some colored pencils and create a key for yourself. I get pretty detailed because I'm a facts girl. I like to know when she's sleeping, eating, playing (out of crib), set in crib, happy in crib, fussing off and on, mild cry, crying, and screaming. This helps me picture how the day went. I don't track every meal throughout the day, but I do measure when I feed her around sleep times. It's helpful for me to know how many times I fed her in the night, and whether she went right back to sleep afterward. I also needed to know how the crying went-- whether she was just rolling around in her crib calling out every few minutes or actually crying really hard. You'll notice that I document every hour in the day, which may seem like overkill. But it doesn't take long, and documenting every hour helps me to discern patterns and see that my baby really is happy most of the time.

56

Some apps provide charting similar to this, but I find there's not as much detail as I'd like, and paper and pencil is still easier for me than entering data into my phone.

If you're doing a modified-cry version, you can also track when you went in to console/for how long. This is important because your subjective memory sucks when you're sleep training. Listening to your baby cry for 10 minutes can feel like an hour. Plus, you can look back over a few days' data to see patterns and improvement.

Even if you're doing a no-cry option or you're not wanting to fully start sleep training yet, a sleep log is super helpful to track your baby's natural patterns. You will be able to see roughly when he goes down for each nap and about how long he sleeps. After you see a pattern develop, then you can more easily set a specified time for naps and help him get on a schedule that you know will work for him. I can't tell you how much freedom I felt knowing what time my girls needed to nap every day and being able to plan my schedule predictably. Hallelujah!

Here's a blank version for you to use and my sleep logs from when I trained my oldest and youngest babies. I sleep-trained my first two children right at 5 months, and my third and fourth I sleep trained at 4 months. Keep in mind, with my first, I was totally winging it and I realize now I made some big scheduling mistakes.

Sleep Log

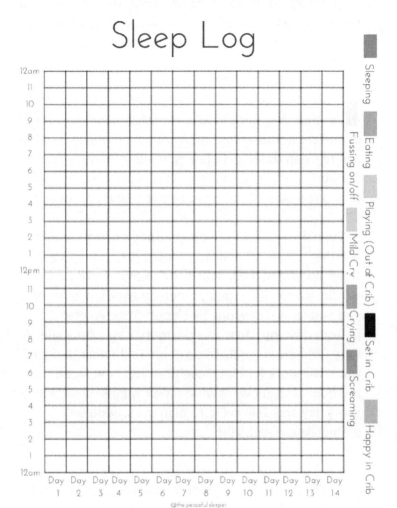

@the peaceful sleeper

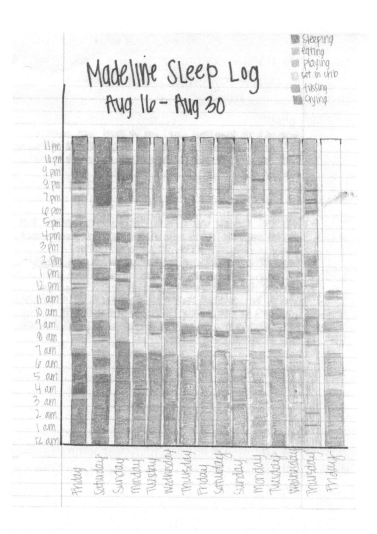

*If you're reading the paperback version of this book, it will be nearly impossible to discern these charts. Hop on my Instagram highlights to see them in color.

Let's dissect this so you see a real picture of how it goes: Sleep training started on day one at the first nap. What I know now is that I put her down for that first nap too late (two hours after she woke up). She would have been happier if I'd put her down 30 minutes earlier. You'll notice that first nap stabilize rather quickly about 90 minutes after she woke up for the day from there on out. The second nap that day was also a little rough, with about 30-40 minutes of crying before she fell asleep. At bedtime she cried for about 30 minutes before she fell asleep that night too. (It's funny because until I pulled this out, I would have told you she cried for over an hour that first night. See, this is why charting is important!) She woke up again a little after 10 pm and cried, but I didn't get her and she fell back asleep after a few minutes.

Now, let's look at day two. So much less crying already!! She fell asleep on her own so fast at bedtime that night! She still woke up and cried around 10 pm, but that was short-lived. On day three, she didn't wake up at 10 pm and almost never did again after that. You'll notice that her nap times really developed and solidified.

On day 13 she had a rough night going to sleep. She cried for about 10 minutes four different times before really going to sleep for the night. (It wasn't even that bad--but when you're in the moment, 10 minutes of listening to her cry feels like an eternity. This is why subjective memory sucks.) My exasperated husband turned to me and said, "Babe, this isn't working. What should we do?" "Yes it is!!" I told him. So I grabbed my chart, and boom! There it was. You could see in little colored boxes that there were dozens of times she'd gone right to bed without crying or played happily in her crib before going to sleep. It felt like a huge regression, but this rough night was totally an exception. (And you can expect to have an outlier rough night here and there.) Had it not been for this log and seeing how many good days we'd had, I could have easily concluded that this wasn't working. But I had proof that her crying time was diminishing and her schedule was solidifying. After these two weeks, we shifted bedtime even earlier, to about 6:15, and also had a consistent early-morning feeding at about 5am. Smooth sailing.

On the next page, you'll find my chart from when I sleep trained London.

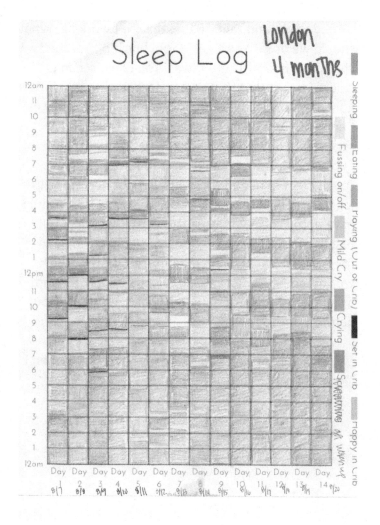

Sleep Log London 4 months

The first thing I notice when I see this chart again is that I clearly knew what I was doing this time. I did a way better job scheduling right off the bat and she caught on with very minimal crying.

The next thing that stands out, is that she did great the first two days and then night three was really rough. I hear this from moms all the time! Don't be dismayed if everything seems to go to crap around day 3-5. Just stay the course and it will get better again.

Notice since she is 4 months she had very short awake times and not super long naps. You can see her schedule solidifying though, so after about a week I could have created a schedule based off the clock instead of only following her cues. This is where the sweet spot happens: when you can map out a schedule that looks the same every day.

Since London is my third, I have bigger kids with set schedules, carpools and activities. I made a separate log of my schedule conflicts, compared that to my sleep log and created an optimal schedule for her that allowed for consistent, uninterrupted naps. It didn't always unfold perfectly and sometimes I had to stretch her awake time or wake her up early, but it was a great backbone to our already hectic schedules. It feels impossible to prioritize baby's naps, but with some creativity and motivation it can be easier than you think.

Does that seem too easy? Maybe your baby has specific concerns or challenges that I haven't addressed. Or maybe you just need someone by your side to help you troubleshoot or answer your questions along the way. That's what consultations are for! I have a wide range of options to fit your needs and budget.

Barriers to Sleep Training

So many things can get in the way of parents sleep training. Let's talk about what those barriers are and how to work around them.

How do I sleep-train?

Well, friend, that's what I'm here for. Hopefully this guide will help you out along the way and answer all of your questions. If you have more questions, reach out to schedule a consultation! I also have a wide range of troubleshooting guides to answer frequently asked questions.

When do I sleep-train?

The ideal time to sleep train your baby is around four months. You'll catch them right when their sleep drive is strongest and they're starting to crave routine. This means they won't protest for long, and they'll pick up on new patterns quickly. If your baby is older than five months, the ideal time is now. The sooner, the better. 18-month-olds are more set in their ways and will protest louder and longer than eight-month-olds. Don't get me wrong--you're never too late to develop good habits. But the longer you wait, the harder it'll be.

You'll want pick a time when you have two solid weeks available to plan your life around sleep. If you're going on vacation next weekend, start when you get home. Ideally, you want to have a good month without major upsets to the routine.

What do I do when I feel guilty?

I hear ya. Listening to your baby cry and not rushing to his aid defies your parental instincts. As parents, stressing out when our little ones are crying is actually a biological response. It's a good thing we have those instincts, but sleep training is one of a thousand cases as parents where we check our instinct against the bigger picture and determine our course of action. While sleep training, we gently and conscientiously push through our discomfort for a purpose.

Many passionate parents argue that assisting our babies when they cry is "an instinct for a reason" and feel that "leaving" our babies to cry is cruel and cold. Please remember that just because something is an instinct doesn't mean that we should follow it, unrestrained. Eating and sex are also human instincts, and we don't need to look far to see examples of how those can be problematic when left unchecked.

But I get it. Listening to those cries feels like torture. Your heart breaks, you feel guilty, you worry he feels abandoned and if you're like me, your anxiety goes through the roof, you can't sit still, and you certainly can't sleep. But that's more about us than it is about them. That's our guilt, not their need. Do you feel as guilty when they protest in their car seat? Maybe, but you push through it because you know it has a purpose. Remember, their needs can be different from their wants. In this case, they *want* to be with you, but they *need* to learn how to initiate sleep independently. Or honestly a lot of times they want and need to sleep, they just don't know how to get there on their own yet. There will be similar frustration when they're close to rolling and crawling. It doesn't mean they're not ready or you're mean for providing space and time for a skill to develop. **There is protest in development and growth.**

It helps to remind yourself that **sleep training is *for* your baby**. When the scheduling is good and baby isn't over-tired, this period of allowing for crying and protest is short-lived. But learning a new skill always comes with moments of challenge and discomfort.

How do I keep my baby from waking the other kids?
Oh, gosh, I've been here too. When Paisley was born, we were living in a two-bedroom apartment, and I wasn't ready to have her share a room with her sister. So she slept in a Pack n' Play in my (well-ventilated) closet for her first 13 months to preserve everyone's sleep. This option worked best for my family.

Depending on the age of your baby, the very beginning of sleep training doesn't usually entail having baby cry it out in the middle of the night. We focus first on baby learning to fall asleep independently at naptime and bedtime and usually unnecessary night awakenings will drop on their own over time. But eventually, to extend morning wake up time or drop some night awakenings you may need to let baby cry while your other kids are sleeping.

If your kids are sharing a room, I'd recommend displacing one of them for a week when you tackle the sleep training challenges that involve crying during sleep times. Big brother probably won't sleep through the wails and may even provoke the madness. Either make a bed for big brother or sister on your floor, or bring a Pack n' Play for your baby into your closet, bathroom, or bedroom. If the baby is in your room, you either need to go sleep on the couch, or you'll need to somehow block her view of you. If she wakes up and sees you, but you still won't get her up, she'll protest extra hard. Even if she can't see you, she may still know you're there, so sleep training with baby *in* your room really is the worst option. If the kids are in separate rooms, get some white noise machines and just prepare your family to power through the next few weeks. They'll learn how to sleep through the crying. You're massively reducing noise and midnight wakefulness in the long run, so just keep the big picture in mind.

Help! How can I sleep-train twins?

When there are two babies in the mix, it's easy to talk yourself out of sleep training. It seems impossible, right? *They'll never be able to be trained because they'll constantly wake each other up.* And what about completely different sleep temperaments? Yep, that happens too. Any way you slice it, sleep training twins is extra difficult! Well, anything with twin babies is more difficult, am I right?

But do you know what's harder than sleep training twins? Not sleep training twins! Twins who don't know how to sleep will keep you up twice as much at night. And if they aren't on the same schedule, you could potentially never leave the house because a baby will always be sleeping. And don't even get me thinking about toddler twins who don't know how to put themselves to sleep. No. I can't go there. That's what nightmares are made of.

While it's harder to sleep-train twins than a singleton, it's also more rewarding. There are some special guidelines when training twins that make it possible.

When you *first* start sleep training, I recommend keeping two sleep logs and following their individual needs for 2-3 days. You may be trapped at home for a weekend because one baby might always be sleeping, but I like to get a picture of their individual sleep needs before we start to make modifications.

Then, we want to do our best to keep them on the same schedule. Unfortunately, in the twin world, the golden rule of never waking a sleeping baby doesn't exist. When one baby wakes, you wake the other one as well so that you can put them down again at the same time. Sometimes your twins will naturally be on the same sleep clock, and other times you will have one twin that seems to need more sleep than the other. Once you know their sleep temperaments, you will be able to make the judgment call on when to let one baby sleep longer.

I recommend leaving the shorter sleeper in the room

until the other twin wakes up (up to 15 minutes). You'll be amazed that she can learn to sleep through the noise of her brother. But sleep, she will. I know it's hard to believe that babies can learn to sleep through their siblings screaming and crying, but I promise you they can!

You can sleep train twins in the same room. Get a noise machine, get a fan, and then probably get another noise machine, and they will be able to sleep. Helping twins learn to sleep is hard, but I promise it won't be as bad as you think. Sometimes things will go even better than expected.

I live in an apartment. What if I wake up the neighbors?
I am all about being a courteous neighbor, but remember to prioritize your children. Bake the neighbors some cookies, write a note, apologize profusely, but tell them you are sleep training, and they'll hear some extra crying over the next few days. There are some great white-noise apps they can download for free to minimize how much sound they'll hear. But at the end of the day, living in apartments sometimes means hearing your neighbors' noises, and that's just something we all have to deal with.

Again, the bulk of the intervention is happening before naps and bedtime and only rarely involves cry it out in the middle of the night, so your neighbors should be fine.

What about teething?

This is another huge reason I advocate for sleep training a baby at about four to five months old. Usually he hasn't started teething yet, so you can get him to be a great sleeper before that teething wrench is thrown in. When he is sleep-trained but teething, you'll usually hear a wail at night, and he'll fall right back asleep on his own. If you suspect teething pain, give him some Tylenol or teething tablets if you'd like. Baltic Amber Teething necklaces can be helpful for reducing pain, although it's not recommended to let a baby sleep with it around his neck. You might try wrapping the necklace around baby's ankle instead in footie pajamas, so he's still wearing it, but in a safer place.

When your baby wakes up in the middle of the night while he's teething, let him cry for a few minutes before you go in. Usually, he'll fall back to sleep on his own. If he doesn't, give him a quick snuggle, nurse if you have to, and put him back in bed. You don't want to create a night-waking habit. If you accidentally do (if it's been more than a week, it's likely becoming a habit), let him cry it out for a night or two, and he'll bounce right back to the old routine.

Here's another place where a video monitor is helpful: If your baby is just rolling around in her crib moaning, she's not really calling out for help. If she's sitting up or standing and looking around the room for over a minute, she wants you to come in. More often than not, she's just uncomfortable, but she's not asking for you.

What do I do when she's sick?

Sickness inevitably comes, and it will wake up your little one in the middle of the night because she's feeling crummy. I'd give her a minute or so to feel it out before going in, but if she needs you go to her. Again, video monitors are super helpful. If she's rolling around and moaning, she probably doesn't need you. I can't tell you how many times I've mistakenly gone in at the first peep when one of my babies was sick, and she's disoriented and looks at me like, "What are you doing in here? Put me back in bed!" She didn't actually want me--I just jumped to action because I'd been woken up. Give your baby the love, comfort, and medicine she needs, and she'll bounce back to the normal sleep routine in a few days. If she doesn't, let her have one night of crying it out once she feels better. That should reset her.

What if I think she's hungry?

This one is by far the trickiest! And honestly, mama, you'll know better than I will if your baby is actually hungry. Once he's two to three months old, let him get a little worked up before you feed him at night. This serves two purposes: 1) He'll actually be awake enough to get a good meal in. 2) If he's not that hungry, he'll fall back asleep. This teaches both of you to discern real hunger. Once he's four to six months old, he still may need one or two nighttime feedings, but not more than that. After six months, if he's sleep-trained and can fall asleep unassisted, he should be able to last eight to 10 hours or more without eating. (This still means you'll probably have one feeding at night). If he can't go for that long of a stretch, you may want to consider supplementing his nighttime bottle. Otherwise, you may just have a habit of midnight waking that you can let him cry through.

If he cries for longer than 40 minutes during one of these midnight wakings, I'd go feed him. Remember, most babies have a wakeful period around 5:30 am, but they'll fall back to sleep if you let them. I held onto my first two babies' early morning feeding until they were about nine to 12 months because I figured they were legitimately hungry. My youngest two dropped their dawn feedings on their own at 6 and 7 months.

What if sleep training turns out to be so stressful and/or disruptive that it's not even worth it?

I get it. You're in a rhythm. Sure, it takes up to an hour to put her down sometimes, or you wake up a few times at night, but it's fine. Maybe she's in bed with you, and it's not ideal, but you're used to it. Everybody's (relatively) happy. I've been there. It's quicker and easier to just bring her into your bed so everyone can go back to sleep. But what's easier now will be harder in the long run. Find a way to commit to sleep training even when you're dead tired in the middle of the night. I promise those rough nights will be over before you know it.

In my method, the meat of sleep training is in the scheduling. And since we start off with CIO during the day, during naps and at bedtime, it's not usually all that disruptive. Once baby has gotten the hang of initiating sleep you can tackle night awakenings if you need to. Usually they'll drop those naturally, but if you need to intervene and help baby drop an awakening you can. Let her cry for 20-60 minutes when she wakes up before going in to feed her. I like to mute the monitor and set timers for 20-minute intervals. When the timer goes off, I simply check the monitor. If baby is crying hard, I'll go in. But if she's fussing on and off, I'll reset the timer to give her a chance to try and fall asleep on her own. If, after 40-60 minutes she hasn't fallen back to sleep, feed her and put her right back down. Babies will usually drop a night feeding after a week of this if they're not waking from legitimate hunger.

Yes, this part feels disruptive. It's easier and quicker in the short run to just feed her and put her back down. But in the long run there are way less tears and way more sleep. You may just have to fight through the anxiety and your temporary sleep loss because you know this pain is very short-lived but entirely worth it.

We have SO many bad habits. Where do we even start?
   This is a good question. Generally, I recommend focusing on one thing at a time in order to ease the transition for your baby. Start by getting her in her own bed in her own room. Then, start prioritizing sleep and establishing a predictable routine. Ensure early bedtimes and early naptimes. After you have those things set, then work on helping her fall asleep unassisted. Sometimes it's easiest to focus on scheduling and preventing over-tiredness first and transition to their room/crib at the same time as CIO for sleep initiation.

You choose!

Self-Care

Taking care of yourself is a gift to the whole family. Self-care can be relatively quick and easy, but it shouldn't be neglected. You function better when you've taken care of yourself. Pinky swear.

I wouldn't do the therapist in me justice if I didn't take a second to emphasize how important self-care is. You know that saying, "if mama ain't happy, ain't nobody happy"? It's the truth. Moms--don't neglect yourselves!!! Sorry for yelling. I know the work you do in and out of the home is divine and important. But it's certainly not easy. Take a few minutes to brainstorm activities that make you feel relaxed and content. I'll wait.

Seriously, stop reading and think of some things.

Surfing the internet is great and all... I do it too. But it's rarely rejuvenating. Worse, sometimes it puts you in a downward spiral of thinking everyone else on the planet has their sh*t together and you couldn't even get a bra on today. I won't tell you to abstain from social media because then I'd be a giant hypocrite, but just make sure that's not the only mental break you give yourself throughout the day.

Find joy and peace in the little things. Sometimes you can add meaning to really simple, accessible experiences. For example, when I first started my career, I had a super-stressful job in a drug treatment center. I was on a big grapefruit kick at the time, and I started this ritual that really helped me de-stress. When I was feeling overwhelmed by my job, after work I would come home and peel a grapefruit while watching a show (*Gossip Girl*, to be exact) in a bubble bath. I dunno, somehow the warmth of the bath, the cold grapefruit, and the methodical process of peeling off all the little white pieces created this great mindful moment for me. My point is, you don't have to hire a sitter, take a whole day off, and spend a ton of money to create some "me time" to practice self-care. Look for simple ideas!

Other ideas:
- There are two apps called "Calm" and "Headspace" that have tons of cool free meditations and relaxing sounds
- Dan Siegel is a mindfulness researcher--he's the man. He has awesome free mindfulness meditations you can find here: http://marc.ucla.edu/mindful-meditations
- Eat a pomegranate (also slow, methodical, and delicious)
- Go on a walk
- Stretch
- Go to bed early
- Have lunch with a friend

- Go to the gym
- Do your hair and make-up
- Paint your nails
- Go on a date
- Go get a massage (here in Vegas we have these "Foot Spas" that will do a 60-minute full body massage for $20. Don't mind if I do.)
- Call a friend
- Start a hobby or craft
- Find a therapist--Don't feel like you need to have major issues to benefit from therapy. It's so great to just unload to someone every once in a while and strategize together. Friends, moms, and sisters aren't always the most neutral parties to discuss certain topics with. Issues feel much smaller when you've said them out loud to someone and have received validation and encouragement in return. I love going to therapy for my own well-being, and I love working with clients for these "maintenance" kind of sessions.
  Search psychologytoday.com for a therapist in your area. Or reach out to me if you're in Utah, Texas, or Nevada and are interested in online or in-person mental-health counseling.

What do you do for self-care? This isn't a rhetorical question. Actually sit down for a minute and ponder this question. It's an important one. Think of things you would realistically do that would make you feel rested and rejuvenated.

I went to an awesome seminar a few months ago by the creators of Tiny Habits (www.tinyhabits.com). They did an incredible exercise with us that I'd encourage you to do here as well. You can modify the principle for any area of your life that you want to make a change, but we'll use self-care as our example.

First, grab a stack of sticky notes and write out 20-30 ideas of how you could practice self-care (one idea per sticky note). Next, arrange the sticky notes top to bottom, based on how much you think that idea would actually benefit you. For example, if I'm brainstorming, I might come up with an idea like gardening that may be relaxing, but might not be *as* good for me as, say, doing a girls' night once a month. I like to arrange the sticky notes on my counter or on the kitchen table so I have lots of room. The most impactful self-care goes at the top, least impactful self-care goes at the bottom. *Note: once you're settled and your hierarchy feels right, you're not allowed to rearrange top to bottom anymore.

Next, start moving the sticky notes left to right, based on how likely you are to actually *try* the self-care idea. Be realistic with yourself. It's usually very easy to come up with a list of things we *should* do, but let yourself acknowledge that there are many "shoulds" we put on ourselves that we simply aren't likely to do. For example, I love to read. I often set a goal to read for leisure every night before bed... yet I rarely actually do this. Such ideas get moved to the left. The ideas that I know I will likely implement get moved to the right.

What you end up with when you're done is a cluster of three to five sticky notes in your top right corner. These are the activities that would both be really good self-care and you're likely to actually do. Just concentrate on those three to five activities and let the other "shoulds" go. This doesn't mean the other ideas aren't important, or that they're "shouldn'ts" now. You can do as many of those as you'd like to as well. But if you're focusing on adding more self-care to your life, that top right cluster will give you the most bang for your buck.

Another favorite tool of mine in therapy is to make a list of all the things in your life that need to get done. Then, on a separate piece of paper make three columns and add the items from your first list where they belong:

- I do it
- Someone else does it
- It doesn't get done

These are the only three options we have.

What I usually find is that there are way too many things in the "I do it" column. We have expectations of ourselves that are far too high and they overwhelm us. There's too much frustration in the "someone else does it" column because we either hate asking for help or we're fed up with spouses or kids not pulling their weight. And there's too much guilt in the "it doesn't get done" column.

I challenge you to set more realistic expectations for yourself. Accept your limitations and make peace with the fact that you can't do it all. Powerfully choose to put more things in the "it doesn't get done" column and move on.

Sometimes you'll serve Cheerios for dinner. Sometimes "cleaning" your house means frantically throwing stuff in the hall closet. Sometimes your kid shows up at play group with dirty feet and pizza sauce on his shirt. It's fine. It's all fine.

Your 14-day plan

You've arrived! You've done your reading, you understand the theory behind sleep training, and you're ready to jump in. You have two solid weeks ahead of you to plan your life completely around your baby's sleep schedule. You don't have to stay home all day for these two weeks. In fact, I encourage you to get out! Schedule playdates with friends, socialize, go on walks, play at parks, etc. But you do need to be home for nap- and bedtimes.

Please note, your baby will have her own unique sleep tendencies. The following guide is meant to give the average parent and baby some general direction. Tweak it as necessary, and reach out for individual consultations if you need to. As much as I wish I could write the one-size-fits-all guide that answers every mom's questions... Unfortunately, there's no such thing.

For the sake of ease, I'm going to assume that your baby is four months old. If your baby is older, your average protest times will be longer, but you also won't have to play the "is she hungry?" guessing game in the middle of the night, because the answer is probably no.

Day 1:

This is it! The moment we've all been waiting for. Sleep training begins today! You have some anxious energy and some butterflies and apprehension. That's okay. You're going to be fine. Everyone is going to be fine!

Baby wakes up at 5:30 am ready to PAR-TAY! She's wide awake and looks so happy and cheerful. "Hi, baby girl. Ooooh, Mama loves you so much!" It's not time to wake up yet, though, so grab that baby a bottle or a boob, feed her, and set her back in the crib. "Night-night. It's not time to wake up yet. It's still sleepy time." And you close the door. One of two things happens now: either she gets offended and upset that she was just put back in her crib and starts to protest, or she just coos and plays happily in her crib. You start to second-guess yourself. She did, after all, just wake up from sleeping all night. "She's probably not going to fall back asleep yet." If she's happy, leave her be. She'll surprise you and fall back to sleep on her own. It might take 30 minutes, but chances are really good that she'll fall back to sleep. If she doesn't today, don't lose hope. 5:30 am does *not* have to be your baby's wake-up time. If she protests a lot, wait five to 10 minutes and go back in there and soothe her. (But don't nurse again, because she just ate. We don't want nursing to become a crutch.) Tell her again that it's not time to wake up yet. After 10-15 more minutes you can go back in and soothe her again. Repeat this process as much as necessary, but I'd be surprised if your baby protests hard for very long first thing in the morning.

When your baby wakes up around 7 am, greet her with big, warm smiles and an excited "good morning!!" If she never fell back asleep, you can get her out at 6:30 or 7.

Eat some breakfast and play for a little while. Notice how active your baby is, and also notice when his activity level slows about 60-90 minutes after waking. He's still happy, but he has longer moments gazing at something. You might even catch a little yawn. That's your cue. It's naptime again. On day one, err on the side of caution and plan on naptime earlier than you think it needs to be. There's way less protesting when your baby goes down too early than when he goes down too late.

Go back to your baby's room and do your naptime routine. Our monitor has a lullaby on it that I love. It's the perfect sleep cue. So I turn on the lullaby, turn on the white noise, close the black-out curtains, sit in my glider, and read some stories. Then I feed her if she's hungry and then rock to sleep. On day 1 we just want to set the stage for a well-rested baby. So rock to sleep like you usually do and try to get all naps to be at least an hour long.

The top priority for your baby's first nap on day one

is that he actually sleeps. You're setting the stage for him to be well-rested tonight. So if you have to resort to whatever you did before to get him to sleep, that's fine for today. We can ease into this a little.

It's important for you to really understand this: We are NOT making baby cry it out for naps on Day 1. CIO starts at night on day 1, after a day of good naps.

While your baby is sleeping, shower and get yourself ready for the day. When she wakes up, it's time for an outing! Whenever she wakes, greet her with big smiles and lots of excitement. You want her to be able to recognize the excitement of awake time vs the quiet of naptime. Go do something fun and interactive. Again, recognize her activity level when she's awake and playing energetically, and also notice when her energy starts to wane.

Your baby's second nap will probably be sometime around noon. Do the same thing you did for his first nap. In my experience, the first nap is the easiest, the second one is slightly harder, and the third (and fourth) nap and bedtime are the hardest. This is because it's easier for him to become overtired later in the day.

Once bedtime rolls around, between 6 and 7 you may have the advantage of your partner being home. Make sure you've both read this guide so you're on the same page. I like to have the longest bedtime routine here. Bedtime is a sweet time, so enjoy it.

If you are doing strict CIO, after your bedtime routine and your last feeding, leave your baby's room planning not to return until 60 min of crying or a regular middle of the night feeding. Hopefully baby will fall asleep within that hour, but if not, you can go in and soothe to sleep at that point. Keep track of how long the crying lasts, but also find a way to emotionally separate yourself from the crying. It's torturing you, but your baby is fine.

If you chose modified CIO, a timer is critical. It will feel like an eternity, but timing is important to maintain consistency. If he cries hard, return in 10 minutes. Console him until he calms down, then tell him again that it's time to go to sleep and walk away. This time leave him for 15 minutes before returning to console. If he's still hollering, go back in and console him again after 20 minutes. Repeat this, at 20 minute intervals 2-3 more times, and then go rock to sleep if need be.

Please know that if you do strict CIO, your protest time will be about half as long as it would be with a modified version, meaning most babies will protest 30-60 minutes on night one. Alternatively, if you choose a modified-CIO approach, you may let your baby cry for 10 minutes, console her for three minutes, cry for 15 minutes, console her for three minutes, cry for 20 minutes, console her for three minutes, cry for 20 minutes, console her for three minutes. If you count up the time, you're already at over an hour.

Emotionally, strict CIO feels harder for parents (and maybe babies) those first few days, but it's faster and easier after that. The tradeoffs may or may not be worth it to you.

Middle of the night feedings: I find that most babies hang on to a 10pm and 4am feeding until about 6 months, and then just a 4am feeding until around 7-9 months. Sometimes there's a 1 am feeding thrown in there too, which will hopefully drop naturally very soon. In the beginning of sleep training, we're just going to feed baby when she wakes and not do any crying it out in the middle of the night. (Unless baby is waking up more than every 3 hours.)

Day 2:

The biggest difference on day 2 is that now we are doing CIO for naps as well. Pay careful attention to sleepy cues and keeping awake times before naps nice and short. And this time, after your naptime routine leave baby to CIO the same way you did last night.

Many parents ask me if they can do strict CIO at night time but modified CIO for naps. You can try, but I prefer to be consistent. If you want to do modified CIO for naptime, just make sure you keep the intervals nice and long. It's important that baby not get over-tired here. So if your little one protests for an hour, go in at that point and rock to sleep.

Babies younger than 6 or 7 months can't really afford to miss a nap because their over-tiredness will build up and subsequent naps will be harder. So if your babe is little, rock them to sleep, nurse to sleep, or do whatever you need to do so they can catch a little sleep here. Don't dismay. We have more chances to get the hang of it.

Babies older than 9 or 10 months might not soothe to sleep at this point. Give it a shot, but if it doesn't work just get baby out of bed and try again for a nap in an hour.

Day 3:

Day three may look exactly the same as day two. Don't get discouraged! We set aside 14 days for a reason. Hopefully you'll see some progress, though. You'll notice a little less protesting, and you'll start to be more in tune with the lull in your baby's play, signaling she's ready for her nap.

Day 4:

Holy cow! She went right back down this morning after her dawn awakening. And she woke up at 7:30 cheerful and ready to play. Okay! This is starting to look promising.

The first nap rolls around. She had a lull in her play, and you caught it immediately! "Time for bed, Little Lady." And what's that? No protesting for her morning nap?? Amazing!

You may still have some protesting for later naps and bedtime, but the first nap of the day will start to get fairly easy.

The biggest change you'll notice is that the protesting starts to drop off when you initially put your baby in his crib. He'll play nicely in his crib for a little while, but he still may cry before falling asleep. If you're doing modified CIO, only start your timer for consolation once he's really protesting hard. He may holler on and off, but don't go in to console him until he's been consistently crying for ten minutes.

Days 5-7:

Keep on keepin' on. All in all, protesting is diminishing, and you're starting to recognize patterns throughout the day. Be prepared for hiccups, though. This is normal! Some nap- and bedtime protesting may persist and feel similar to that of day one. Some babies *totally* unravel on day 5. I don't know why, but just try again tomorrow.

Days 7-14:

Take a moment on day seven to examine your data from the past week. What might have felt scattered and random before will hopefully make more sense once you can see it all on one page. After seven days of data, you'll realize you're in more of a groove than you thought you were. Hopefully your baby has dropped the night wakings that aren't tied to legitimate hunger, and even though she may still protest a bit, it's pretty minimal.

Remember, with modified CIO or with older babies you may not see this much success yet. There will be improvements, but you're probably not seeing sleep initiate without any protesting yet. You *are* going in fewer times to console, though. Despite all your successes, you'll still have some episodes that undermine your sense of progress. Stay the course! You are well on your way to having a sleep-trained baby. And believe me, life gets *so* much sweeter when your time with your baby is full of play and enjoyment--not continually coaxing him to sleep.

Days 14-30:

Your baby can now self-soothe and fall asleep on his own, so now you're figuring out your ideal schedule and letting naptimes solidify. The exact times he goes down and wakes up may vary slightly. Ideally, you won't have more than a 30-minute variation in either direction, though. You may still have some days with a little bit of protest before sleep, but nothing like it used to be. Just like learning to walk, you'll still have stumbles. That doesn't mean he isn't getting the hang of it. It just means it's not perfect yet. Focus on maintaining consistency and planning your life around this new schedule of yours. There's a lot of freedom that comes from knowing exactly when his naptime will be—but you'll also need to be diligent about keeping those times free and clear of other obligations to preserve sleep.

One common hiccup parents still experience is the nap-intruder, or what I often refer to as the "crap nap." This is when baby only sleeps for 30-40 minutes when, ideally, we want to see naps lasting longer than an hour.

Your two main interventions here are:

1. Adjust awake times: If baby is waking up after less than 45 minutes, he is likely going down for his nap too early or too late. I generally err on the side of keeping awake windows short. So try shortening awake windows first, and then lengthen them.
2. Leave baby for 30 minutes after awakening to try to fall back to sleep.

Focus first on getting baby to learn how to fall asleep independently. Then, a week or two after you sleep train you can tackle nap lengthening.

If you need more help here, refer to my "Crap Naps" troubleshooting guide found on my website, www.thepeacefulsleeper.com

Have a Life While Preserving Baby's Sleep

Of course, having a baby throws off your social game a little. But keeping baby's sleep sacred doesn't mean you have to be stuck at home all the time.

I'll let you in on a little secret: having a baby who is sleep-trained actually opens up a whole new world of freedom and flexibility. As you've already learned, the key to success and ease with sleep training is preventing overtiredness at all costs. So yes, you do need to plan your life around that little bundle of joy and his sleep times to some degree. But! The beauty of sleep training is that you know exactly when those times will be.

Step 1- Get your baby sleep-trained and maintain predictability.

This means (give or take 30 minutes) you know when your baby is going to need to sleep. This gives you *so* much freedom and flexibility because you basically know your schedule every day. Plan to be out and about while she's awake, and plan tasks at home while she naps. (I've never felt trapped at home while my baby naps because I always have a mile-long to-do list that never quite gets finished. If you're a typical mom, I bet you do too.) Find friends with babies the same age and plan playdates. It's likely that their nap schedule will be similar to your baby's, which makes socializing easy.

Try your best not to mess with sleep times, especially in the first few months. Don't keep your baby up later than he needs to be or rely too much on him getting his nap in the car. Don't count on him being flexible with naps until about 12 months. At that time, when his sleep has become predictable, he can handle going down an hour later on occasion. But in those early months, throwing off naps can wreck the whole day, sleep-wise. Then one funky day can lead to another. So, it's best to just stay as consistent as possible.

Step 2- Get your gear and make plans for nap- and bedtime outings

Once you've had a pretty established sleep pattern for about a month (with your baby at home in her crib), you can start to get creative in order to take trips and be out of the house at bed- and naptime. By then, your baby can get used to sleeping elsewhere. My three must-haves for sleep on the go are: <u>Pack 'n Play</u>, baby monitor (<u>audio</u> or <u>video</u>), and <u>white noise</u>. Some Pack 'n Plays come with all kinds of bells and whistles that are quite unnecessary and cumbersome to haul around. Get a simple one that's easy to transport. <u>Travel Pack 'n Plays</u> are lightweight and very convenient. For maximum ease, I prefer a <u>video monitor</u> that doesn't require wifi. You can set it up instantly wherever you go, without having to get any login information. I have an awesome <u>white noise machine</u>, but you also can download a free white-noise app on your phone. If your baby likes a paci, stuffed animal, or blanket, bring those along too. I always pack the same bag and fill it with the same five things. It takes three minutes.

Once your baby's routine has become predictable, she'll go down almost anywhere if the conditions are right. I've literally done this hundreds of times. There have been times a friend has planned a potluck lunch at her house right in the middle of our naptime. Instead of saying "no," I'd ask if I could put my baby down in a spare bedroom, well-ventilated walk-in closet, or bathroom. Most everyone will have a quiet place a baby can sleep (the darker the better). Other times I've arranged lunch with a girlfriend while both of our kids are sleeping. I'll bring take-out, we'll put the kids down for naps, and then we can just hang out. If I have an appointment I don't want to bring my baby along to, I'll schedule it during naptime so I can drop her off with a friend. Asking if your baby can sleep at someone's house is basically a non-request, since there's no actual "babysitting" required.

The biggest social event to navigate with a sleeping baby: hanging out at night. It's easy enough to keep naptimes clear of social engagements, but when your baby goes to sleep at 6 pm, it can really make for an early night on the weekends. Our solution: usually when we hang out with friends, we grab dinner and then go to someone's house to watch a movie or play games while our baby sleeps in a quiet room there. If it's not possible to do dinner with the group early, either my husband or I will stay behind at my friend's place with the sleeping baby while the other goes to dinner, and we'll all hang out after. It's not as weird as it sounds to hang out at your friend's house while your baby is sleeping and wait for everyone to get back. Come on, you know how to surf Instagram for an hour. This brings me to step three...

Step 3- Host more!

Guess what? Even when it's easy to transport your baby around and have him sleep in a Pack 'n Play elsewhere, he's still happiest in his own room in his own crib. Host more. Offer to do game night or dessert at your house. Plan potluck brunches with friends. You don't have to have the biggest or nicest house in the group. And it doesn't have to be spotless either. No one cares. Just invite people over!

Step 4- Find great babysitting options

If forking out tons of cash for a fancy babysitter isn't really an option and you don't have the luxury of having family close by, don't fret! You have options! If your baby is sleep-trained and (hopefully) has an early bedtime, this opens up a world of possibilities because you can still start your date night at 6:30 when your baby is snoozing at home. Look for young babysitters who don't charge the big bucks, and put your baby down before they arrive. I personally think 14-year-old babysitters are the best. They're so eager, and they actually play with your older kids and bring activities. Or if you just have the one baby, you're paying a sweet young girl to watch Netflix at your house (and maybe even unload the dishwasher). If the entire job takes place while your baby is sleeping, I allow the babysitter to bring a friend so they can still have a fun night. I usually pay $7-10 an hour if they're under 15.

My go-to option for years was date-swapping with friends. I'd babysit for them on Friday night, and in return they'd babysit for me on Saturday. When my oldest was a baby, I'd just go over to my friend's house, set up a Pack 'n Play in her closet, and go on my date. Asking a friend if your baby can sleep at her house is such an *easy* request. When it was our turn to babysit, same thing. They'd bring their baby over, put her right down, and then the hubs and I would watch a movie and eat popcorn, forgetting that we were even "babysitting."

Another option is for one of you go to the friend's house to babysit while the other stays at home with your sleeping baby. Then your baby can stay at home in his crib when it's your turn to go out. This is convenient because the babies are still going to bed in their own cribs and don't have to be woken up to go home. But it does mean that one night of the weekend you and your partner won't be hanging out together. But the payoff is that it buys you a free date night and the babies are happy, so for me it's worth it.

Sleep Training long term

Will there be relapses? Yep! Lots of them.

Sorry to burst your bubble. Life happens, and there are several factors that will disrupt your baby's sleep after she's fully sleep-trained. The good news is, these natural upsets will be temporary. Once she's sleep-trained, it's pretty easy to get back into your rhythm if you know when and how to do it.

One big advantage of having a sleep-trained babe is that you can discern when there's a real problem that needs your attention. If your baby wakes up in the middle of the night or is unusually upset after going down, you know it's worth checking out because it's out of the norm. For the most part, even if you did strict CIO with your baby during sleep training, you're fine to take a "Check and Console" approach in situations like these.

Unfortunately, sometimes babies become accustomed to night waking after illnesses or other legitimate reasons for waking up at night. Generally speaking, I give up to a week for an illness or teething to take it's toll. After a week, you run the risk of enabling a bad habit when your baby usually isn't suffering at all anymore. (If she is still sick or teething, then by all means, keep going in at night.)

Things that might wake up a sleep-trained baby:

- Sickness
- Teething
- Overtiredness
- Bad dream
- Poopy diaper (babies usually won't poop in the middle of the night, but if she pooped right before she fell asleep, she's likely uncomfortable)
- Leaking diaper
- Daylight savings
- Noises (neighbors, a dog barking, or a car alarm)
- Lost pacifier or comfort object
- Legs stuck in the bars of the crib
- Sleep Regressions

Note: after your baby has been sleeping through the night, hunger will not be a real cause of arousal

How to tell if a sleep-trained baby needs you at night:

- Baby's demeanor while crying
- Length of cry
- Frequency of waking

Again, video monitors can be quite helpful in discerning needs during night wakings. If your baby is old enough to sit or stand, but when she cries out at night she's just rolling around, she probably doesn't need you. She's most likely still asleep but just experiencing a bad dream or some mild discomfort. If she's sitting, standing, or looking straight at the monitor, she probably wants you to come in. The tone of her cry will also give you clues--if she sounds quite distressed or like she may be in pain. If you're questioning whether or not you should go in, give her five minutes, and if she's still crying, go see what's up. Or, if she falls asleep again within those five minutes but wakes up two to three different times throughout the night, there's probably something going on.

After the hiccup has passed, you really just need a night or two of crying it out before she'll bounce back to her regular routine. For a well-sleep-trained babe who has only been out of her sleeping-through-the-night habit for a week, this shouldn't be more than 10 minutes of crying.

If there aren't any specific signs of what's causing these night awakenings, and they're pretty consistent for a week or so, with your baby just moaning and rolling around, my guess is that he's overtired. Bump his bedtime up 15-30 minutes, and that should do the trick. Otherwise, it may be one of many very normal sleep regressions. Weird stuff happens to babies' sleep when they're on the cusp of some developmental milestone. Sometimes they'll have a huge sleep spurt, where they're taking three-hour naps and sleeping late into the morning. Or sometimes they'll have massive sleep regressions and fight sleep for a week or so. Just stay the course, be consistent, and they'll bounce back.

A final note:

Many first-time parents wonder when it's time to take a pacifier away or try to wean thumb sucking. For sleep's sake, don't rush it. I would hold off on doing any of that until your child is three years old or has stopped napping. The last thing you want to do is take away a self-soothing strategy for an older babe who has been using it her whole life. Our little gal took a tumble once that jammed her sucking thumb, so she proceeded to stop sucking her thumb completely, even after it felt better. That created the WORST 6-week sleep regression known to man. We essentially had a 2-year-old who didn't know how to self-soothe anymore. It. Was. Awful! My husband, the dentist who by profession wanted her to kick the habit, was praying she'd figure out how to suck her thumb again. She eventually relearned how to self-soothe, and thankfully everything went back to normal. But my point is, there's no need to subject yourself to a massive sleep upset for no reason. When your little one isn't napping anymore and generally has pretty good sleep habits, you can start to figure out a plan to wean her from pacifiers and sucking her thumb.

Conclusion

Congratulations! You now have a fundamental understanding of sleep training. You know the theory behind why sleep is so important, and you know how to optimize your baby's sleep in a way that is short, effective, and protects secure attachment. Parenting isn't easy, and your little one's sleep habits will throw you for a loop from time to time. But you won't be thrown off your game, because you know how to bounce right back to your regular routine.

You know that your number-one tool for good sleep is preventing overtiredness. You know that enabling consistent sleep times and sleep environments for your little one is crucial for continuing success. And most importantly, you now understand the methods to implement all of that.

Your next step is to get to work. Figure out your plan and your optimal time to start, and go for it! Remember to use a sleep log to track your progress. You've got this, mama! In no time at all, your baby will be sleeping blissfully, and you'll feel a renewed energy that you didn't even realize you'd lost. I'm looking forward to that for you. It's such a good feeling when something that was previously stressful no longer is.

Please keep in touch! Follow me on Instagram

@the.peaceful.sleeper and share my page with your friends. I post sleep tips constantly and have free Q&As on Instagram Live. If you need individualized help, don't hesitate to schedule a consultation. I have a whole range of coaching options and some smaller troubleshooting guides to fit your individual situation.

Tell your friends all about what you've learned, and send them my way!

And above all, happy sleeping!

xoxo,
Chrissy

Resources

Jackson, D. (2003). *Three in a bed: The benefits of sleeping with your baby.* London, UK: Bloomsbury.

McKenna, J. (2007). *Sleeping with your baby: A parent's guide to cosleeping.* Washington, D.C.: Platypus Media.

Pantley, E. and Sears, W. (2002). *The no-cry sleep solution.* New York, NY: McGraw Hill.

Perlis, M. (2016). *CBT-I Principles and Practice Basic Course* [Presentation]. University of Pennsylvania.

Sears, W., & Sears, M. (2001). *The attachment parenting book: A commonsense guide to understanding and nurturing your child.* Boston, MA: Little Brown & Company.

Sears, W., & Sears, M. (1993). *The baby book.* Boston, MA: Little Brown & Company.

Turgeon, H., & Wright, J. (2014). *The happy sleeper: The science-backed guide to helping your baby get a good night's sleep.* New York, NY: The Penguin Group.

Weissbluth, M. (1999). *Healthy sleep habits, happy*

child. New York, NY: Ballantine Publishing Group.

Made in the USA
Monee, IL
15 August 2021

75715392R20069